Rhymes For No Reason

by

Joy Thacker

ISBN 0 952176 02 5

Copyright Joy Thacker, 1999

Published by Joy Thacker
Fairhaven
Whiteway
Stroud
Glos
GL6 7EP

Typeset by Qwertyop, The Vatch, Slad, Stroud

Designed and Printed by
B. A. Hathaway, Nailsworth, Gloucestershire

Rhymes For No Reason

There must be a grain of reason in a little book like this,
In its thoughts of things to tease on - in events to reminisce,
In its different views, unusual slants, in humour, comments too,
In the laughter which I hope it brings, with a knowing smile from you!

The book it is the product of a filler in of time,
Not researched, ordered, structured, and scrutinized by line.
Not in command of anything - just merely of my mood,
Then all thrown up, and tossed about, with hope it will be good!

Most ideas came within the night when the good are all asleep.
Around the hour of three or so into my head they'd leap!
They impinged upon my daily toil, so I could get no peace
Until sole abandonment for them gained me welcome release!

The ideas first astounded me, I'd never thought this way!
They caused me to think differently, my instincts to obey!
They caused me to delve deeply, to unravel things around
Those simple things like genders - and worms deep underground!

Please read me through, so you might judge that what I say is sane.
My indulgence not excessive - that I should have refrained!
That my credit and my counsel would be best left to myself,
Or the door creaked open further for more volumes on your shelf!

CONTENTS

FAMILY OBSERVATIONS 3

Grampy's Cottage: An Ode to Katy	5	Foods with Go!	13
Her Bedroom	7	Chimney Sweeping	14
Mother's Cat	8	Her Loss	15
Keith Thacker is a Character	9	Baldness	16
Eating in our House	10	Henna	17
A Breakfast Ditty	12	Our Car	18

THE BATTLE OF THE SEXES 20

The Snorer	23	A Man for Every Purpose	28
Men and Women are Different	24	The Collecting Mania	29
Mr Perfect	26	My Addiction	30
The Make-Over	27		

ON THE PERSONAL SIDE 35

The Cup and Saucer	37	The Antiques Roadshow	50
Wine-making	38	I am a Vegetarian	53
The Wine Glass	40	Supermarket Shopping	54
Rodborough Common	42	Money	56
A Little Culture	44	Gloucestershire Quirks	58
Browning's Milk Round	46	Hilda	60
Holidays	48	My Friend	62
Butlins	49	My Forgetfulness	65

PURSUITS 69

I am a Water Diviner	71	All Wrapped Up	82
No Pleasure in Things Anymore	72	The Crazy World of Up and Down	84
The Common Cold	74	The Garden	86
The Bed	76	House-plants	88
The Hot-Water Bottle	78	Cars	90
The Telephone Directory	80	Super Hints	92

Body Parts 97

A Mirror Never Lies	99	The Stomach	106
Hair	100	Bottoms	107
Eyes	102	Feet	108
Tongues	103	The Itch	109
Chests, Bosoms, or Busts	104	Skin Cells	110
The Heart	105		

Livestock 115

The Invader	117	The Earthworm	124
Flies	118	A Little Bird	126
Germs	120	The Rat	128
Nits	122	Fish	130
A Dog Tale	123	Fox and Hounds	132

Miscellaneous 137

The Lavatory	139	Dreams	148
The Toilet Roll	140	Grass	149
Hoses and Pipes	142	The Force of Gravity	150
Mr Dustbin	144	Not The Bitter End	152
Light	146	The Last	153
Time	147		

ACKNOWLEDGEMENTS

I should like to thank all those who in a variety of ways have contributed towards this book *Rhymes For No Reason*, including Anthea Mundy, proofreader, Rod Shaw, typesetter, and Barry Hathaway, printer, for their help and enthusiasm. Also I thank my family and friends for their interest and their patient listening through endless recitations, and all those who have given encouragement, some unknowingly, through my memories of them in past times. Outstandingly however, and he must head my list, my heartfelt gratitude goes to my husband, Keith. He has not only given me enormous support but also, with unselfish forbearance, has allowed me to use the experience of over thirty years of marriage to inspire several rhymes. For this ultimate sacrifice my gratitude knows no bounds!

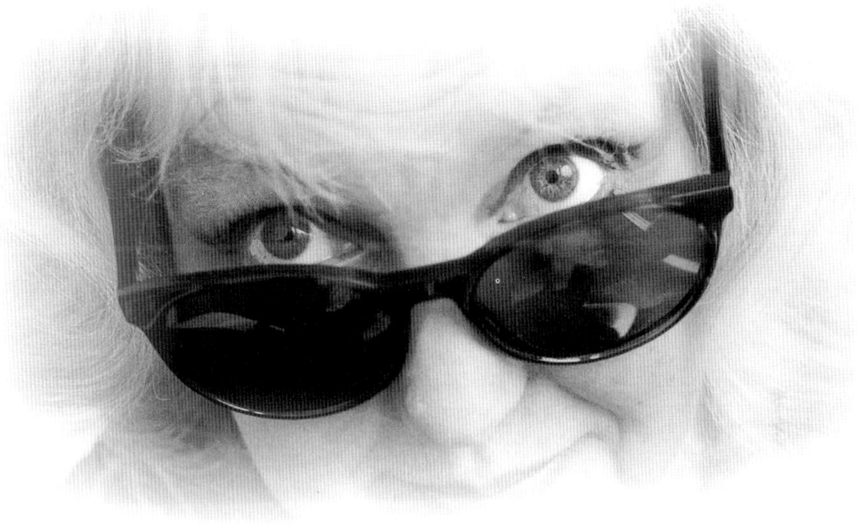

Family Observations

For the following citations, family members should be thanked
For all the inspiration gleaned from those within their ranks!
That without the visual image of one member, we should note
The existence of some poems would certainly be remote!

'To know one, you must live with one', is how the saying goes,
Which really means quite quickly you will learn their cons and pros!
It is a pity when the cons can push out precious pros,
Just why this often happens - no one really knows!

Put simply, it really means small annoyances increase,
We tolerate them, as we do, to retain some form of peace!
Eventually they grow and grow until something must be done,
As we rant and rage, to reach a stage of mutual solution!

Habits become attached, entrenched, when practised over years.
Change is disliked when new pursuits are clothed in dread and fears!
To smarten up their looks they hate, or to throw old things away,
And when faced with this prospect, dug-in heels they will display!

The best way to accomplish change is through the water test,
You start a year or two before - the drip will do the rest!
Eventually if all goes well a miracle might occur,
But usually it takes some time - I've found it can take years!

Another way, not welcomed, is through doing it yourself.
It is not liked, not by an ounce, so wise people use some stealth!
It is not thought as cowardly when things are rid while they are out.
In fact it is the best way - for health suffers when we shout!

Those who have coped with families will know the truth I speak,
That to alter them is hopeless however hard you seek.
In fact it's often when we stop, things seem to turn out right,
Then you ask yourself - why bother with the hassle of a fight!

Grampy's Cottage: an Ode to Katy

The cottage where my daughter lives was my Grampy's 'til his end;
   He lived there with his family before it was condemned.
It was quite small, but he and they were happy and content,
   It's good that it remained unchanged until the old pair went.

It became updated as required and made to look brand new,
   It gained a modern bathroom, a pink bath and a loo.
The kitchen range was ripped out, a gas heater there installed
   And the panelled doors which caught the dust, replaced by some hardboard.

The cottage windows, paned and quaint, were modernized, updated.
   The old front door so dark and drab was sanded and repainted.
The front-room fireplace (old and large), replaced with something small,
   The rugs which once had reigned supreme, were rid for wall-to-wall!

The large old table was removed for a sixties kitchen set.
   Large wood-armed chairs for settees – more comfort and more rest!
Brass bedsteads swapped for low divans – no chance to hide beneath,
   No need too for potties for quick midnight relief!

The garden, which gave fruit and veg, gained shrubs and flowers galore,
   The old wood seat where Grampy sat, removed from by the door.
The old wash-house, where hens were plucked, made superclean and neat,
   No room within this modern home for Grampy's hobnailed feet!

Katy arrived so bright and young – she loved it at first sight,
   So she set about restoring it to what she thought was right.
She installed a reclaimed fireplace – she did it all herself,
   Then she sorted out those hated doors, and all those modern shelves!

(Continued overleaf)

The kitchen lost its modern feel when the units disappeared.
    It lost its modern gas fire, too, as a wood-burner appeared.
    The larder used for pots and food was reshelved and reclaimed,
Only those things original were permitted to remain.

On Sunday mornings, Kate rose bright to visit the car boot,
    To buy some chairs, a settee, other things she thought would suit.
Thick curtains to be hung at doors, thick velvet in rich hues,
    A brass bedstead, a counterpane, paintings diverse, profuse.

The attic which had not been used she boarded for more space,
    A spiral staircase was installed to reach up to the place.
The nooks and crannies this produced she used to full effect,
    Some held her books, some hid high-techs, not one did she neglect!

The garden over two years was transformed beyond belief,
    If Grampy could just see it now he'd tremble with relief!
It still has lawns, flowers, and some shrubs, but a mass of veggies too,
    And new fruit trees, and seats to sit to enjoy the marvellous view!

New windows were the next to come – they were custom-made to suit.
    Next year the new trees planted will yield first time their fruit.
One day there'll be another room above the scullery,
    Old Grampy would have liked all that with his large family.

Some people who saw all of this were shocked and thought it strange,
    But they are now converted to Kate's inventive range.
She has shown us that things we dislike need not remain always,
    Should we, just like that Katy, wish for a past heyday!

Her Bedroom

Her bedroom was a perfect place done out in girly pink,
   Of matching curtains, carpet, walls, and other things to link.
But shortly we knew we were wrong when she told us both one night
    That what she really wanted – was a bedroom black and white!

It took a while to make the change, her carpet last to go.
   I did regret the need to change, – but how was I to know
When it was finally finished, quite stark with all replaced,
    She'd decide to move on and out into another place!

The home she now inhabits has warm colours soft and kind,
   It could not be more different from the room she left behind.
Her room here still retains white walls, although long gone is the black,
   A perfect empty background for my hoard of bric-a-brac!

Mother's Cat

Mother's cat has survived ten lives yet they seem a whole lot more
When from a tiny kitten she was never on the floor.

Instead on shelf and ceiling, on lampshade and up wall,
It really is a wonder Kitty has survived at all!

A time when Kitty could have died was the day she nearly drowned
Within the toilet basin where a lid had closed firm down!

A call of nature saved poor kit, as she struggled to prevent
A nasty journey down a pipe of a none-too-pleasant scent!

Another time she nearly was the meat meal of the day
When Kitty chose a warm oven to wile her time away.

Her mewing and the need to bake stopped a frizzling which would be
A smelly, messy business – and not one we'd wish to see!

She's older, fatter, wiser now as she kills off mice and birds,
Then brings them in so proudly, to our condemning words!

Her actions cause me fury as she gloats midst feathers, bones,
And it's then I think an eleventh life might just fail to bring her home!

Keith Thacker is a Character

Keith Thacker is a Character, it's seen within his clothes,
It's seen within his beard and hair, and his askew nose.
It's seen within peculiar gait, within demeanour gruff,
Within his voice which can be brusque,
                when few words are enough!

He is not tall, he's rather short – stocky with sturdy legs.
It might be said he's overweight – the outcome of beer kegs!
He does not mind what people think – his clothes reflect this trend,
They're holey, torn, with zips all broke –
                long past the urge to mend!

He has a pair of hobnail boots, which once were 'down in pit'!
He proudly wears them out on walks, to pound and crunch on grit.
He has a treasured garage – too large, too full, a mess!
It is the source of arguments –
                and matrimonial stress!

His wife she is a patient soul – she's born her burden well,
For thirty years she's coaxed, cajoled, despite a life of hell!
She once thought she would change him, 'He might succumb, just might!'
And faithful to her ideal,
                she maintained a fruitless fight!

But deep inside she now admits she never will succeed,
Dog types like him do never change – it's inbuilt in their breed!
So Keith remains a Character content in disarray,
Just like a dog and long in tooth –
                his habits are to stay!

EATING IN OUR HOUSE

If you should eat within our house you would know variety,
   Not here the same old boring foods of perfect constancy.
     Not here a fare of haute cuisine at each and every meal,
No, here food is thrown together according to how I feel!

    So we'll celebrate variety, wild surprises every day.
    A chance to taste a unique mix combined in no sane way!
    No sameness, and no surety, things mixed in with a wish
    To make the final product an experience not to miss!

We do not measure anything with scales, or spoons, or cups
   To take away the pleasure of a dish which just erupts!
     The same ingredients might go in, but the result is not the same,
Tell me who wants to eat a meal which is perfect, dull, and tame?

    So we'll celebrate variety . . . .

I did once measure recipes to a formula set and tried,
   But it did not suit my attitude when it took away the pride
     Of making something I was sure no other person had,
Which is sometimes mediocre – but at other times not bad!

    So we'll celebrate variety . . . .

An example of haphazardness are meaty pies which can
   Be herby, hot and tasty, or mild as a young lamb!
     Crisp biscuits can be very crisp, bread moist just like a cake,
A fruit cake very gooey – this just happens when I bake!

    So we'll celebrate variety . . . .

I'm lucky those who eat food here accept me as I am
  And not feel disappointed when a filling's curd not jam!
  When a fork used for a thick rich soup will laugh at a mere spoon,
And teeth wonder by the minute of whatever else might loom!

  So we'll celebrate variety . . . .

I was a cook for several years - did training and all that.
  Sat those exams, had been precise, and got it all off pat!
  But it took away the thrill when I knew that each dish would turn
    out right,
So I took to ad hoc cooking, and my world again was bright!

  So we'll celebrate variety . . . .

A Breakfast Ditty

His Friday morning breakfast is the highlight of his week,

When he with mates at half-past eight meet up to eat their treat

Of a Trucker feast, which doubles up on foods fried, and not fat-free,

Which is well helped down with toast and jam, and a pint mug full of tea!

Should Friday be a holiday, his morale is very low

When his wife does not cook or approve foods which can make bellies grow!

So he braves the day without a word, until alone on motorway

His car veers into the Services and a fried breakfast leaps his way!

Foods with Go!

The prune, baked bean, and parsnip too, are labelled from their birth
As foods of some mean ridicule, as subjects of great mirth!
From digestive tracts, are wind effects which folk wish would cease to grow,
So not mention in society, although society does know!

The fig has got a similar role, can we mention bowels here?
As have the cabbage, sprout, beetroot, to keep our systems clear!
Rhubarb will also do the trick – but avoid that bowl of bran
Unless you wish to face next day as a worn out also-ran!

A counteractive remedy is several hard-boiled eggs
To bind you all together, and save those poor tired legs!
Old people suggest blackberry tea – port, others recommend
Which will cheer up all those innards when they feel they need a friend!

Chimney Sweeping

Sweeping day within our house was upheaval, mess and fun,
Well that was for most everyone excepting poor old Mum!
Mum was the one who cleared the decks, washed down, and put things back.
Her wish was not to see the brush come out the chimney stack!

The day was usually drab and cold even when in Spring,
Sweeping was usually Saturday when we tackled the whole thing!
It all began quite early so that cleaning claimed the day
For washing walls, fresh curtains, and to chase the dust away!

Me and my friends said we would help: 'Please can we beat the rugs?'
Mum said we could, so we hauled them out and walloped them for bugs!
When we were tired we packed that in for the 'tumpt' where we could see,
The brush burst from the chimney like a monster spider, free!

As it emerged we chanted loud, 'It's out, it's out, it's out!'
Dad came outside to check himself – could he have any doubt?
The brush emerged about three times before it disappeared,
Without mishap which we would like – but father always feared!

From then on all was very tame, our sweeping game was dead.
So we wandered off to leave clearing to the capable instead.
Soiled paper was picked up inside, the floor swept, brushed and scrubbed,
The carpet laid, the brasses cleaned, wood things waxed and rubbed!

After the sweep we hoped for warmth and no need to put fire in,
After all we were in April – it was meant to be the Spring!
But invariably as the eve drew on and a slight chill caused us pain
In came the kindling and some coal, and we had a fire again!

The saddest part of all this lark is when a swept fire emits smoke,
When wisps like tiny tendrils veil the room as with a cloak!
Then past phrases are aired again, 'It's the wind, it's in the east!'
And, 'At least the room is clean and fresh – but next year we'll sort the beast!'

Her Loss

Across the dance floor she saw his smile, he asked her for a dance.
She said she would and they shuffled round,
it was the start of their romance.

She fell for his teeth, his white, white teeth, his crimped, smart, thirties hair,
But shortly after marriage,
they had gone - to her despair!

Her loss is very real today, 'False teeth were not the same.'
She talks about his balding pate,
'A few hairs did remain!'

Their demise she blames on many things, but she's glad one thing remained,
'He never lost his lovely smile -
that always was the same!'

Baldness

As one blessed with a head of hair I'm intrigued about the fate
    Of heads where thatch is sparser – I'm talking of bald pates.
Most of these heads are covered up for the best part of the year,
    So extent of hair is hard to gauge when it never does appear!

Do bald heads feel exposure to heat or cold on top?
    When the rain comes down, does the naked skin feel every single drop?
If there is no hair, no strand even, is the head washed with the face?
    Or is it shampooed carefully, as if lack is some disgrace!

Do flies and insects land on top because a hairless head is smooth?
    And struggle to retain their hold, and slide off when bald heads move?
Do bald heads feel more vulnerable, do they flinch and do they sweat ?
    Does rain drain off them easily to make a neck and collar wet?

Do bald people live more cheaply without shampoos, cuts or brush?
    Is it quicker to get ready when no hair aids the rush?
Are large beards grown to compensate? Most bald men have a beard
    Which is curly and abundant – when there's none on top it's weird!

Another thing I must ask about is the one of potency,
    Is it really true that sparse-haired men have a heightened adequacy?
That baldness is a visual sign of a fervour simmering strong,
    Which is why those virile, ardent, men do not keep their hair too long?

I would like to do a survey of those who have no hair
    With those who have a headful, to see how they compare!
For us women it is merciful we are not viewed in this way,
    Or we'd all wear scarves or even shave, to attract the men our way!

Henna

For those who don't know henna, it's green but turns out red,
It's an ancient form of colouring which can be used upon the head.
It looks just like a powder until mixed in a paste,
Then it looks and smells like cow's muck – but no, I don't know how it tastes!

I first came across henna, when my daughter was thirteen,
She wanted her long thick locks to have a reddish sheen!
We applied and worked the mixture – we did get in a state,
But we found out very quickly that things stain at a fast rate!

My hands were red, and so were hers – there were streaks which caused her tears,
There was paste along her hairline, and it was clogged within her ears.
It took some days for the hue to fade from those parts meant not to tinge,
And we learned at cost to wipe it off before it could impinge!

We were bad friends for a little while, the water was too hot!
I'd stained across her forehead, and on other countless spots!
But in the end when all calmed down the colour looked just fine,
So I was then allotted to henna her another time!

Now I'm a henna expert I know just what is what,
I always don my rubber gloves like a surgeon in an op.
Her head I clamp with a plastic bag so the stuff will stay contained,
And leave the rest for her to do – so I don't get the blame!

Our Car

Our Standard 10 black family car was strong and built to last,
   There was a lot of space inside, and it had some sort of class.
It shone a lot, when it was cleaned a lot, by someone who was proud
   Of its sunshine roof, which leaked at will,
                         And a horn which croaked out loud!

On visits to our Auntie's the large back seat was fine
   For sleep on homeward journeys, or at any other time.
But its yellow wheels when older, were more than we could bear
   As we purred slowly up Gloucester Street
                         To the policeman standing there!

At last it went for just ten pound – a waste at any rate.
   But in those days we cared not a jot as we roared off in Morris Eight!
But those early memories firm remain, of tassled holds and running boards
   On which we rode, though told not to,
                         So it did have some reward!

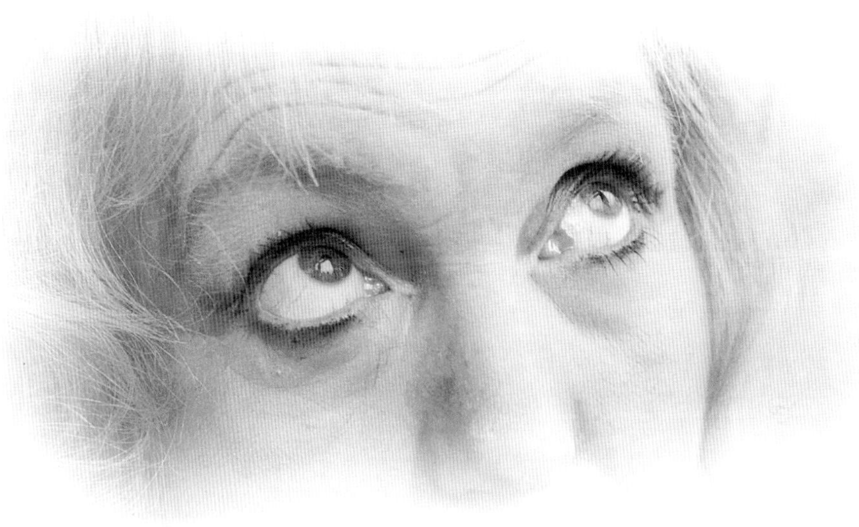

The Battle of the Sexes

People of different genders are spread throughout the earth,
They occupy all nations - sex determined at their birth.
Often it's hard for them to see the other's point of view,
Which they can talk of easily, but always fail to do!

The poems which now follow are about the wish to find
People who match harmoniously in attitude of mind.
Folk who conform in ways and deeds to another's personal quirks
Which they think, perhaps wrongly, will cause relationships to work!

No two of us will ever think the same about these things,
Some will still crave security, some, freedom with no rings!
Some claim male prerogatives - others fight for women's rights,
Some put complete equality as high within their sights!

It could be modern attitudes which has caused this to occur,
This clash between the genders, the roles of him and her!
Women who work, with their own means, today won't tolerate
The incompetent or selfish man - the one of second rate!

So perhaps these rhymes are biased, when it's women who aspire
To a modern change, of role and range, to claim all they require.
The men, it seems, quite naturally, wish to leave all well alone
To continue on traditionally where women stay at home!

Yes, emotions can run high on this - criticisms fly around
As men refuse to leave their male-dominated ground.
Because of this they receive a miss by the women who will choose
Someone who'll slot in her pre-planned plot, to share, care, and amuse!

So it seems we've reached a deadlock, but we've all been there before,
This gender difference is a whole vast issue for people to explore.
Up till this time, unsuprisingly, no solution seems to be
Because men and women always - will think differently!

The Snorer

I'm married to a snorer, he's worsened over years.
He started in a small way, when he held no dread or fears.
His sound was then quite gentle, a reminder he was there,
But when it boomed to a roaring lion -
then I started to despair!
Those in bed with a snorer, will know what it's about,
It means no chance of sleeping, and the tendency to shout!
Sufferers begin in similar ways - like nudging with the toe,
But eventually when it's all too much,
resentment starts to grow!

People will offer their advice; like balls slipped behind backs!
To prop on many pillows so tubes will not be trapped!
To keep mouths closed, use noses, 'the throat vibrates you know!'
Take tonsils out and adenoids,
'and that dangly bit should go!'
They suggest things seen in papers, like metal clamps on nose!
Pincers to flare the nostrils, and gags to keep mouths closed!
A choice of operations, some drastic, or a pill,
But the best cure for us partners -
is simply just to kill !

Yes, the plastic bag and rope round throat, are tempting in the dark,
When as the clock strikes two, then three, you're fed up with this lark!
'Oh let me get some sleep!' you groan, as the lion starts to roar,
So you thump the beast, and wake him up,
and thrust him out the door!
The salvation of our marriage was the day our daughter left.
Her room nearby was vacant, to enormous benefit,
For the very moment she moved out, he was persuaded in next door,
And at last I slept a deep, deep, sleep -
while he enjoyed his snore.

Men and Women are Different

The book I read the other day has opened up my eyes,
It's about our gender differences – now they're a big surprise!
It made quite clear both sexes think in ways diverse in range,
What men consider right for them – for women is quite strange!

 It seems a man's a thinker, he works his problem out.
 The woman is a talker, she chatters hers about!
 The man to solve his problem will slope off to his cave,
 The woman plunges down her well, and his affection she will crave!

The man he does not want help – it will damage his morale!
He will seldom ask assistance, not even from a pal!
To emerge triumphant from his cave from a problem he has solved
Will raise him high in manliness and give him new resolve!

 The woman does not understand his need to work things out,
 She chases him into his cave to thrash the matter out!
 She'll sit outside his cavern door to coax and to entice,
 But this is wrong, by all accounts he resents her good advice!

When plunging down her narrow well a woman craves his love,
She wants it as she travels down, not shouted from above!
When all her pleas remain ignored and her journey stays solo,
She bounces on the bottom, and resentment starts to grow!

 The way towards your partner's heart is apparently not through food.
 It might assist the process, but praise will do more good!
 When men feel good, they are to us but putty in our hands
 To cater for our every whim, and do all we demand!

A woman fresh up from her well, is happy, loving, giving,
She'll try to do most anything for the man with whom she's living!
She'll care for him, and cuddle up, and chat and chat some more,
Until his cave it beckons peace – in he goes and locks the door!

This might explain why men play golf, and they have garden sheds,
Why they adore their football as much as shapely legs!
Why fishing, cars, and drinking are important to their lives,
These might all sadly indicate – a very noisy wife!

    Women on the other hand do not shut themselves away.
    They remain within the real wide world where emotion they display.
    When they are down, then they are down, when feeling
                                          up they're grand,
    Why men have trouble seeing this, I fail to understand!

To try out this new theory, it was tested out through trial,
We respected all its aspects, and peace reigned for a while.
But soon the boring happiness annoyed to cause us pain
So I tidied up his cave a bit, and we rowed and fought again!

    I stormed off down my well alone, my damaged pride to nurse,
    He tried to come to comfort me, but I found he made me worse!
    When I came up I sought my friends and we discussed at length at tea,
    Then he came in, and we made up, now we're as happy as can be!

*(Inspired by MEN ARE FROM MARS, WOMEN ARE FROM VENUS,
by John Gray).*

Mr Perfect

I'm seeking a Mr Perfect to share my life with me,
  He must fit in with my desires, and allow me to be free.
He must be healthy and go-ahead, with an ambition to match my own.
  He must fit in with my lifestyle – so I won't be alone!

He can be small, not overweight, and fit but not too thin.
  He must have hair which is not grey, not bald or 'receding'!
He should own a house, a car, a horse, some land, maybe a farm,
  With an ancestry which will match mine – of a yeoman with a barn!

When we are wed, I'll keep my name to ensure my family line.
  We'll each retain the homes we have – but we'll divide our time!
We'll meet four times a week, to allow a break to keep the spark alive,
  With passionate love on all these nights so love will bloom and thrive!

We'll share all costs, and my mortgage he'll pay – but I'll keep my bank account.
  We'll holiday abroad as his salary allows – but I'll sort the venue out!
I've decided one child would suit us both – any more would tie me down,
  You see, I must retain some space for myself – for social trips to town!

We'll make separate wills immediately – so my family will claim my estate.
  Not a member of his shall glean a scrap should I die intestate!
If they dared to try to scrounge a bit, I'd rip out their eyes – and more!
  Oh! but I'll be dead, so that won't work – I did not think of that before!

Perhaps Mr Perfect is not the man – I'll forget the whole charade.
  I'll stay within my single state, so things won't be so bad.
This perfect person might be a selfish man – not so giving and generous as I,
  So I think I'll abandon the whole idea in good time before I die!

The Make-Over

My husband needs a make-over to sort his image out,
    He needs to sharpen up his style, decide what he's about.
    To drop a stone, or even three, to get rid of his gut,
To cultivate a hairstyle – he's got rather in a rut!

I like his beard best 'goatee', as Sir Walter Raleigh wore,
    Any waxed moustache like Poirot, I simply would abhor!
    He could do with some new spectacles, with a modern frame
For a clever academic look, to show he has some brains!

His teeth require attention – they seem a little yellow,
    They should be cleaned, capped, veneered, to suit new smiling fellow!
    His skin, I feel, is not too bad, he's getting on you know,
But it would take gallons of cream to make his wrinkles go!

His old clothes I'd like in the bin, but I doubt they ever will!
    It is high time he acquired some more – of these I've had my fill!
    I feel a nice new leather coat would suit his brand new shape,
And trousers which are trim and styled, and do up round the waist!

It's a pity that his legs are short – a defect that must stay!
    Although a pair of built-up shoes may help to save his day!
    Perhaps also a waistcoat would finish him just fine,
In satin, maybe Burgundy, like well-matured old wine!

It's a pity canes are out now, (those with the silver tops),
    He would, I feel, look rather good when striding to the shops!
    On second thoughts, canes would not work, they'd be a perfect pest,
Balanced on a shopping trolley they might prod and cause arrest.

At least I'm here to back him up and never criticize,
    To boost morale when one is low I feel is very wise.
    These people who tell everyone of faults and this and that,
Should resign themselves as I have done to a pale blue bobble hat!

A Man For Every Purpose

I think a man for every purpose is a wonderful idea,
Someone to cater for my needs, exempt of legal seal.
A list of men quite qualified for anything required,
From a fun trip to the theatre, or to get the house re-wired!

My social man will dress real smart, be tall, and lean, and fair,
He will hold my arm, and open doors, and pull for me my chair.
He'll buy me perfume, chocolates, flowers, and see me to my door,
And if I really liked him, a little kiss could be in store!

My sporting man will be toned up through work-outs in the gym,
He'll accompany me in different games and always let me win!
We'll eat together sensibly of foods which are advised,
And we will walk, and climb, and talk, and take some pony rides.

The man who is most practical will sort my home for me,
He'll investigate my wires and pipes, and mend the old T.V.
He'd climb upon the roof to stop the leaking by the eaves,
And check the gutters out for blocks, and make them clear of leaves!

My counsellor man will listen well to all my tales of woe,
He'll give compassion and advice, as emotions start to grow.
He'll hold my hand and stroke my hair, whenever tears appear,
And console me that some things are worse than those things which I fear!

The one who'll have the hardest job will be the stand-in hubby,
He'll have to put up with my moods which are sad or very bubbly!
He'll have to love me very much with an overt adoration,
And praise and do all what I say without the leastest hesitation!

These form, I think, the backbone of my perfect new lifestyle.
There are no ties to keep them – they're just names within a file.
But should one accidentally Jack of all these trades become,
I'd quickly sack the others and make him number one!

The Collecting Mania

My husband has a mania, he collects most anything
Phone books, and newspapers, to lino, knobs and springs!
Rusty bedsteads, mouldy carpets, varied car parts by the score,
Spare shoes and leaky wellies, broken bags and so much more!

I should have guessed when we first met that he was quite a squirrel,
His garden shed stuffed to the brim should have warned this silly girl!
Been wary when he thought our lives would be sadder should they lack
A childhood pair of rabbits – with ears all stuck and cracked!

At first our small loft housed the lot, then he put down extra boards,
Soon some cupboards took some more as he began to hoard!
Then he built up a garage vast with a lofty room on top,
An enormous fabrication in the name of a workshop!

He's widened into music now, and in photography,
Recording from the tele, using high technology!
On holidays his camera lens sees my back view more and more,
As fed up with the snapping I stalk off to explore!

At home we've two recorders, with a system so advanced
That an evening out is planned ahead so as not to miss a chance!
It's said it is the female whose toilet takes so long,
But here it is my husband – as he checks things won't go wrong!

Where will it end I ask myself, nothing departs that I throw away!
It goes into the dustbin – but appears again next day!
Each week when he goes shopping, boxes come in vast array,
He promises to take them back, but once they're here, they're here to stay!

I thought of a great fire to burn away the lot!
I dream of rows and rows of skips to fill with all this rot!
I've told him straight, if he dies first, I'll not preserve a bit,
I'd get it swiftly shovelled out – while I just gloat and sit!

My Addiction

I'm addicted to house clearance, shops with the old and new,
It began when I was collecting cups, but the fascination grew.

Now when I've got some extra cash, and sometimes when I don't,
    I nip to see what's there for me, and if I will or won't!

I usually will, and that's the risk of venturing inside.
There's always something there I like, and it's so easy to decide.

Sometimes I go for what I need, sometimes I nurse a doubt,
    Only today a cloth I craved, but an umbrella stand leapt out!

My home is packed with many things which go back to the past.
I pick them up, and dream my dreams of who possessed them last.

A little pair of children's shoes of earlier decades,
    An old brass vase, a sugar spoon, and fringed ornate lampshades.

The modern things I once so prized make way for something old.
The rocking chair, beloved so much, is an outcast in the cold.

Instead that smaller nursing one for my affections fast is heading,
    While just last week I saw a treat of some old Victorian bedding!

No! my acquisitions are not rare, hardly affluent antiques.
They form instead a nostalgic thread in uniqueness and in creaks.

I stroke each one, and sniff, admire, their form, their charm, their style,
    And vow each day to stay away from those shops - just for a while!

Another real attraction is possibly the price,
Compared with expensive modern things its cheapness does entice.

Now tell me where else a box of books can be bought at little cost?
Or a set of spoons, a music box, or draughts with no piece lost?

Admittedly buys can lack sheen, but cleaning them is great.
They might require attention, but their price reflects this state.

Bits can be lost, they might be chipped, but the choosing's up to you
As you delve into all sorts of things of which you've not a clue!

I think I'll leave it for a week or two then an hour or so I'll spare
Just to browse about, not fork cash out, in some small shop somewhere.

I won't be tempted, for this venture is to break my hunting spell
So I might be completely free from this most delightful hell!

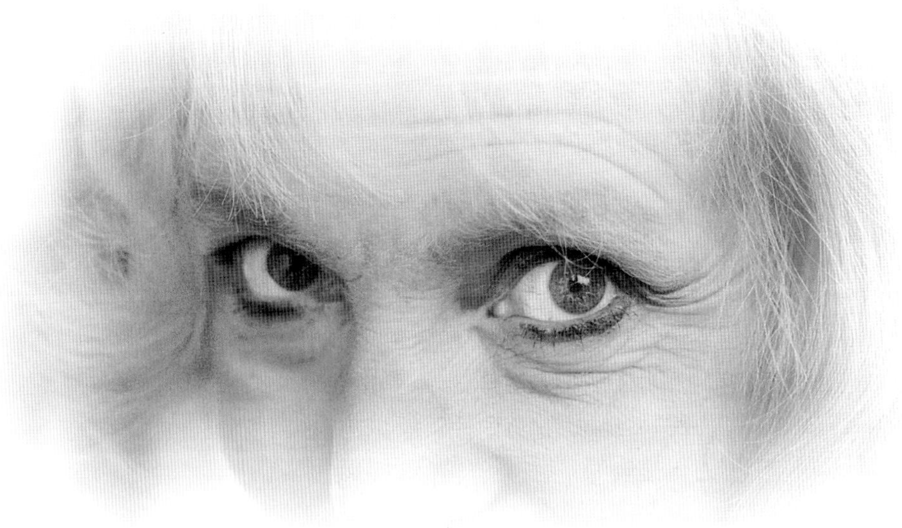

On the Personal Side

The poems which now follow, give a personal view of things,
Some dressed well up in humour, some have a truthful ring!
Some tell of childhood memories, things precious to my mind,
Some others may just seem plain daft – they're a mixture of all kinds!

On reading through them lately a picture has emerged,
Of a freedom fresh erupted, which poetry has served.
A therapy, an expression, a need to tell the world
Of this diverse view of ordinary life which newly has unfurled!

The people whom I write about are all unique to me,
They're my source of inspiration, they've allowed these eyes to see.
When they are set before me, my imagination's fired,
The problem is that unless I'm checked, I can run a little wild!

It's the simple things which can inspire and give out all the glow,
Such as supermarket shopping, or my favourite Antiques Show.
Like wine-making which can go wrong, and those silly childish thoughts
Which all combine to make this part a compilation of all sorts.

The Cup and Saucer

Come back our cup and saucer, where have you gone these days?
    We hardly ever see you, to enjoy your diverse ways.
You once were indispensable for cups of tea each day,
    But now we have large clumsy mugs which have settled in to stay!

A cup and saucer to take tea is what everyone should try,
    They make the humblest occasion a time to linger by!
A table set with lacy cloth, cups, jug and sugar bowl
    Will warm the very heartstrings and reach the inmost soul!

Tea bags have helped this dreadful change – they have rid us of the leaves,
    Those little bits upon our tongues which we spat out as we pleased!
Strainers and slop bowls are not known now, and so are never heeded
    When teabags demand to be squeezed with only two spoons needed!

A comparison with today's lone mug is hard to contemplate.
    In any eyes this coarser pot is a thing of second rate!
With no saucer to catch the drips, white marks will soon appear,
    With no saucer to slurp hot tea, a beloved habit disappears!

A saucer prevents spills on chairs, on clothes, on legs, on mats.
    It will hold countless biscuits – and feed a thousand cats!
When cups are broke, saucers remain – my spare twelve say it's true
    As they enhance my many plants! Is there nothing they can't do?

Tell me where do you put that spoon once you have stirred your mug?
    Where does that tea bag hover, or perhaps your ash and stub?
Those little bits of paper, sweeteners, a choc or sweet?
    With a good old cup and saucer their disposal is so neat!

Tonight I'll search my tea set out – the one inherited from Gran!
    With fluting round the edges, with gold and violets on.
The cups hold less considerably, and drunk with just one glug,
    Which I think it much more preferable, than a dozen from a mug!

WINE MAKING

The brewing which I did for years was learned before I wed,
   A potent family recipe which gave deep sound sleep in bed.
Great Granny had perfected it and passed it down the tree,
   It was a pain each year to make when it was left to me!

The parsnips used were grown by us, twelve rows, or even more,
   We washed then chopped them, boiled them - a liquid gold for us they bore.
We poured this into dustbins where it frothed a magic brew,
   Then after six long anxious months we tried a glass or two!

As the brewing craze took over I made dandy and some plum.
   Some blackberry and elder flower, which gave out quite a pong!
Some carrot, and some beetroot, some marrow, apple, tea,
   Some turned out well, some not so bad - all was O.K. with me!

We bought some remade wooden casks from a Bristol cooper's shop.
   We housed them in the garage loft - they had taps to draw wine off.
We used a yellow Duckhams jug filled to the brim with brew,
   Then drank it dry each evening as our wine collection grew!

When making wine it's difficult keeping temperatures to scratch,
   It's hard to warm large quantities with so much in a batch.
One dubious fermentation lost twelve gallons down the sink,
   It took away our confidence and caused us to rethink!

It was the worst time for us when a bug our parsnip got.
   The wine ceased fermenting properly which infected quite a lot!
We tried to force it down of course - what, waste our joy and pride?
   But in the end it was thrown out - and the grass curled up and died!

The reason why I packed wine in was not to do with this,
    It was the healthy living thing, so I gave that year a miss.
I intended to return to it, not ever just to stop,
    And we did not, because the following week we bought some from the shop!

I miss the sharing aspect of this home wine-making game,
    The washing, mess, and slicing, with sharp knives which could maim.
The blisters and stained fingers, numb feet from concrete floor,
    All of which were soon forgotten as the first glass we did pour!

In the garage waiting patiently the old copper stands today.
    The wine dustbins hold rubbish – but we can throw all that away!
The casks are dry, but a water soak will plim them up just fine,
    So really I have no excuse but to go and make more wine!

The Wine Glass

If I came back as a wine glass, I'd be the high élite,
    I'd attend those grand occasions and be used for special treats.
They'd proudly hold my fine-cut shape aloft for all to see
    So that the centre of attraction would definitely be me!

At dinners and at weddings I'd be pleased to hold the toast
    For this very important visual task and not let down my host.
I'd contain, of course, the finest wine – not your supermarket red!
    What give my drinkers headaches? Well, I'd rather be seen dead!

Wine glasses come in classes, they crave a high esteem,
    They aspire to grace high table – to be the cream of cream!
A well-cut lead does not wish to clink with cheap, thin greens,
    He has a standard to maintain within his public scene!

A high society, fine-cut glass will elude pretentious airs,
    With oodles of fine quality, no vulgarity is there!
Very ably they can hold their own with the highest in the land,
    As the famous, and the royals, grasp them in regal hand!

Wine glasses come in different shapes, in sizes and décor,
    They're exclusive for the drink they hold and the occasion they're there for.
It's certain that a champagne glass will think herself the best
    With her slender stem and shapely bowl, no-one could think her less!

Wine glasses can dislike the wine they're often asked to hold,
    Which can be cheap, or very warm, or sometimes too darn cold!
For a wine glass to endure a wine for which it does not care
    Is the equivalent for a wine glass, of the worst human nightmare!

For the wine itself this attitude can put him in a stew,
    Imagine being jovially slurped from someone not liking you!
In this case tact, diplomacy, is the order of the day,
    As he whispers very humbly, 'I shall soon be on my way.'

But not all our glasses crave a highbrow social life,
    Some do not wish for glamour, formality and strife.
Some prefer the family bosom, the comfort of the home
    To accompany a family meal, or a quiet night drink alone!

The worst thing for a wine glass is really when it's chipped,
    Now what's the use of something which could cut a person's lip?
In this respect the exquisite, fine and cheap at last unite
    As they stand beside each other awaiting their last rites!

When this occurs it would be best if all were smashed to bits,
    At least they'd keep some dignity should it happen at the Ritz!
But as a receptacle for flowers, picked by children when at play
    For a high-class, fine-cut wineglass – it's a sad way to end its day!

Rodborough Common

Rodborough Common above old Stroud is very dear to me,
It is where I spent my childhood, so fearlessly and free.
It is where I went most everyday, with friends or by myself,
It symbolized our hopes and dreams, our future, and our wealth!

We were not scared up there alone - the Common was our friend.
Danger was not considered, so anywhere we'd wend.
The dark did not alarm alarm us - it wrapped us safe unseen
As lights illuminated below, its darkness was our screen!

I've watched the Common's many moods - it changes by the hour.
It can be mellow, meek and mild, or wild, emitting power.
It can be hot with yellowed grass, or sharp with winds that bite,
It lifts the spirits either way, to make the world more bright!

The contour of my Common is a plateau with steep sides,
It's rough-grassed with much thistle and bushes where cattle hide.
The tracks are used by walkers, by riders and the like,
The dips are fine for lovers, and for boys on mountain bikes!

As children on clear summer days we'd wander off to play -
With Shep, water, and Weetabix we'd be set up for the day!
We'd climb the quarry, walk Wright's wall, and jump over the seats,
We'd imagine we were on our steeds, who pranced, and reared - did feats!

The winter was for sledging down below the Fort,
Where the slope was steep and made quite slick as the big boys did cavort.
Brave heros they when from the top they hurtled down with zeal,
As timid girls much lower, with shrieks used lots of heel!

At this time, too, the dew-ponds froze up by the Lonely Tree,
When we were young we'd slide up there, imagination free!
Within our minds we acted scenes like Christmas cards denote,
Of ladies fine in bonnets, muffs – not boots and duffle coats!

In later years the Common was the focus of romance,
Young couples freed from parents' gaze found it their perfect chance
To walk, and laugh and cuddle, in this high world of their own,
Oblivious to all but them, 'til time to venture down.

Last year I walked my haunts again – nothing there has changed.
The wind still blows, the grass still grows, the horses still do range.
The fairy ring is larger now – but it took my wish again
It was a comfort to my soul that my Common was the same!

A Little Culture

It will be hard for you out there to link me with the ballet,
    I'm not the fragile waif-like sort who'd drift off with a gust!
    In fact, most of my friends when told retort, 'Really? Good Golly!',
Until reminded quickly that young folk are steeped in trust!

In Red Cross House in good old Stroud Miss Jackson held her classes,
    She specialized in guiding people to their cultural souls.
    She moulded the self-confidence of quiet little lasses –
Through ballet, elocution, simple basics she'd unfold!

She would have guessed quite quickly that her task ahead was hopeless
    When she espied this tubby little girl who was but me.
    My chunky form and rosy cheeks made the chance of dance incredulous,
It was obvious a stable yard was where I ought to be!

The thing which tempted me to go were idol girls in comics,
    So delicate and envied as they teetered on their points.
    In ballet shoes and stuck-out skirt they leapt, and twirled and frolicked
With some adoring partner with elasticated joints!

I convinced myself my ballet shoes would turn me into Fontaine,
    Before too long I'd be there too performing on the stage.
    The audience would stand, applaud, as I encored a fifth time,
My Prima Donna future would be well and truly made!

But I stopped my ballet lessons three weeks from when I started!
    Mum saw the sense when I begged, 'Please don't make me go!'
    She thought again and decided elocution should be imparted
To instill in me some speech control she clearly hoped would grow!

Elocution did not need a graceful form of body structure,
    The thin and plump could both achieve a rounded vowel or two!
    There was no chance of injury or an internal rupture,
The mouth moved most, no limb movements, or at least a very few!

The elocution lasted a bit longer than the ballet
    I had to practise phrases to make my accent go.
    Peter Picked and How Now Cow got vowel sounds to tally,
Miss Jackson tried with me so hard, but words would just not flow!

Throughout this time I was projected, thrown and then expanded.
    My dialect of Gloucestershire was being pushed away.
    I did not like all that and the reminding it demanded,
So I purposely reverted to the old style when at play!

A piano interest and a lack of zest finished off my elocution.
    Within a week my accents had quite happily returned!
    Culture and me Mum realised a hopeless situation
As I ground my r's and squashed my vowels, and let my words be slurred!

BROWNING'S MILK ROUND

Those years on Browning's milk round were happy times for me.
    They were a time of growing up and responsibility.
The Brownings were all very kind – they put up with my quirks
    As I moaned and laughed, chattered, was daft, each day when there at work!

    I was nowhere nearly perfect, I had some way to go.
        Not through my lack of trying, we hoped some sense would grow!
    But it seemed to evade capture, for just as it got near
        It would slide away for another day, then simply disappear!

Despite efforts to be reliable I was rarely there on time.
    Dad used to call me to get up, and I'd leap from bed just fine!
But from then on time seemed to fly – I was meant to start at eight
    So when our clock chimed cruelly out, I knew that I was late!

    I broke the bottles quite a lot – they were attracted to the ground!
        The dairy and its echo made their crash seem more profound!
    Their sterilization hot, then cold, caused them to crack and cry,
        But whirl them around, immerse them to drown – see they don't
                                                wish to die!

The hard boiled eggs were a sad mistake – at the time I thought it fun.
    Imagine ordering six large brown to find them cooked and done!
The customers were a fine old crowd, they took it very well,
    But I made sure any more cooked eggs would include soft boiled as well!

    Yes, eggs I found quite delicate when they could not take the heat.
        They could not also take a knock, or a fall from the van seat!
    But eggs must all be cracked you know to get at what's inside,
        So I always consoled myself with that when I saw them start to slide!

My feet have not recovered yet from standing in a bowl
    Of hot water, in my wellies, on a floor so icy cold.
The main problem with dairies is they're not designed for heat,
    I bet all dairy workers have chilblains on their feet!

That dreadful winter of 'sixty three was my first up at the farm,
    We took it all just as it came with no outstanding harm.
Our little van coped very well up steep hills, ice, in drifts,
    We did our best to deliver to all – we tried hard not to miss!

    The summer time was wonderful, bright mornings, sun, warm breeze,
        With customers who were so kind and ready with a tease!
    One gentleman watched out for us, to offer wine on payment day,
        But it went to my knees, so I'd take the cash, then quietly slip away!

On long steep paths I was always glad when someone offered to
    Collect their extra milk or eggs to save a step or two.
I liked it when on payment day their money was put out,
    Especially on wet wintry days when only mad milk girls went out!

    No, I still do not like farm rats, or even smaller mice,
        Some perhaps can see their virtue, but to me they are not nice!
    When their little shed was cleared out, I screamed as in a fit,
        But if vermin was around your feet you'd have complained a little bit!

'The rat in basket' escapade was enormous fun for those
    Who put it there for me to find that night when back at home.
I should have guessed some trickery when Michael laughingly
    Said to leave my basket by the door, because Mother might not happy be!

    I left at last and did 'trained' work and stayed within the warm.
        Though I missed those people on the round, and those upon the farm.
    I missed the kindness I had found – tradesmen with whom I'd joked,
        But I still retain these memories which no one can revoke.

Holidays

Why do we go on holiday and wear our poor selves out?
Why don't we just remain at home to laze and loll about?
Why do we shop so eagerly for clothes which we will dare
To flaunt where no-one knows us,
                 but at home will never wear?

For a time before we pack our bags we worry and we fret,
Mostly about the weather – will it be warm, cold, dry or wet?
Any need to take more woollies? Although they say it's hot,
We pack some more, just to be sure,
                 and add a black sun-top!

We wonder if we need some pills to help our airsick fears,
More cream to ease our suntan, though the last lasted for years!
Some plasters just in case of cuts, some more mosquito cream,
Or that thick yellow bath towel –
                 hotels are sometimes mean!

We wonder should we split things in case luggage is lost.
To add some extra underwear should the worst come to the worst?
We question should we take more shoes, 'Will three pairs need to come?'
But they are in there anyway,
                 so we accept that that is done!

This coat simply should not come – shall we pray for sun tonight?
Not even that long evening dress which is so thin and light?
Those thick socks must come out now, so our case will close together,
Now that's the lot, but oh dear no,
                 I've no mac for showery weather!

It would be so much easier to forget our holidays
To throw away the brochures and decide at home to stay.
To save our cash, to calm our nerves, rest safe and sound at home
Where we will get more restless –
                 in our desire to roam!

BUTLINS

For many, many, many years to Butlins we would go
For a week of entertainment, activities, amusements, shows.
    Butlins gave children freedom, we as parents relished ours,
For that was what it meant to us – safety, no risk, no cars!

From the moment we arrived there, we all were on the go –
Carrying belongings in journeys to and fro.
    Investigating chalets, claiming and making beds,
Shopping for food with special treats, before we dared to rest our legs!

The Sunday after Saturday was calm, serene and fun.
The schedule scrutinized in depth to find things for everyone.
    There were discos for the teenagers, and shows for dads and mums,
With games for every youngster, and food there by the ton!

Should the weather there be warm and fine there was a pool outside.
If cold and wet there were a host of other things to find.
    Should we a require a trip 'outside' then we'd jump into our car
To drive to some interesting place, often not very far.

I liked it in the evenings when we shared alone
A drink or two of home-made wine which we had brought from home.
    We two might well be fast asleep as those youngsters free crept in,
So very quiet so as not to hear, 'Wherever have you been?'

Once we took a school exchange, she came to us from France,
She loved the freedom of the place which she used at every chance!
    'In France we not got things like this – I come again next year?'
But worn with responsibility I lied, 'Not coming, dear!'

We have Butlins' photos by the load pushed within a book,
They're got out just occasionally to take another look.
    They're jumbled up in years and camps, so all's a bit confused,
But Butlins was the holiday to keep everyone amused!

The Antiques Roadshow

We went to the 'Antiques Roadshow'
At Westonbirt in the school.
Many others went there like us,
Armed with heirlooms, jewellery, tools.
Granny's glasses were wrapped in newsheet,
Father's pistol so heavy and strong.
Kate's bangles acquired from a car boot,
    And some cake should we wait very long!

    The school was a perfect show setting,
    In grounds which were open and flat.
    There were signs everywhere to ensure ordered care
    For people and cars and all that!
    Guides welcomed us in at the doorway,
    Signs showed us the way to the Hall,
    There were drinks we could buy to assist time to fly
        While we awaited our call!

        Tickets - Silver, Armoury, Glassware
        Determined our queue on the grass.
        We split up to haste any time we should waste,
        And to get all our things looked at fast!
        Some people had queued there for hours.
        Seasoned 'roadsters' had wisely brought chairs.
        As we all waited there, 'antique' stories we shared,
            Single people were soon linked in pairs!

One man told of a Show down in Bristol.
'The queuing was just like it's here!'
'Are we all seen today or do we come back again?'
I asked as a rain cloud appeared!
Halts for filming I soon much resented
Despite they're a 'must' for the Show.
Recording slowed the queue so programme addicts might view
    Rare objects discussed of some note!

    Some objects were valued most highly.
    A pot with a crack – what a price?
    Hopes started to rise for my own shock surprise,
    A hundred or two would be nice!
    The sun shone on us at the table.
    Granny's glasses so prized offered up.
    I wished him to say they were the find of the day,
        But he said that they weren't worth very much!

        'Perhaps sixty when both sold together.
        The last century but not very rare.
        Yes, they are very stout – they would stand a good clout!
        Who's next? Now what have you got there?'
        For me it was all disappointing,
        But Dad's pistol would surely prevail.
        It was from Birmingham town, of some gunsmith renown
            So I was certain with this we'd not fail!

(Continued overleaf)

Oh dear! What a hopeless disaster,
Our pistol was not as we thought.
It was not linked with heroic past ventures,
Not special, and not slightly sought!
A humane killer, I cannot believe it!
What used to shoot some poor sick cow?
The firearms authority would scrap it?
    No value – they might anyhow!

    Our bangles lacked much obvious merit.
    So what if they were very nice!
    The only things bought, not inherit
    What chance they of any great price?
    Silver Expert is now saying something
    They are Chinese, with words of good luck!
    They were certainly worthwhile our staying.
        They were deceiving when encased in muck.

        The glasses are back in their cupboard.
        The 'pistol' again on its hook.
        The bangles are clean, safe in boxes.
        The Show was at least 'worth a look'.
        We watched it last week on the telly,
        I boldly stood out in my pink.
        I was talking away by the dozen,
            You'd have missed me had you paused to blink!

I am a Vegetarian

I am a vegetarian, I never do eat meat,
I do not think it nice, or needed, not even for a treat!
I've been like this for fourteen years, so I never shall return
To eating meat, however cooked,
deep roasted, stewed or burned!

It was the blood which set me off, it was so red and thick.
A chunk of meat upon on my fork made me feel very sick!
This bit had bellowed, slavered, kicked - it was too much for words,
So I left the lot upon the plate,
and fed it to the birds!

I sadly had no moral stance - I would like to say I did,
It was the blood and living bit which caused me meat to rid!
I had no trouble finding food which I liked so much more,
My varied plates of countless veg,
are tasty - not a bore!

I did not try to replace meat, as health buffs say we should,
With endless mounds of cheese and eggs to keep me feeling good.
No, I have eaten what I like - my system's sparkling clean,
Those other people who like their veg,
will know just what I mean!

Supermarket Shopping

This supermarket shopping is a time-consuming game,
You'd think it would be simple, and the whole pursuit quite tame.
    But oftimes such a basic task can turn into a pain
When things crop up to hinder and make us wonder why we came!

You should allow an extra hour on the time you think you'll take
To buy all those provisions – make a list, for goodness sake!
    Include high upon your list a thing not oft considered
That of bumping into long-lost friends – an item rarely figured!

We meet these when we're looking drab with clothes and hair awry.
When we are feeling sad or down and a misword makes us cry!
    When we would rather shrink and die should it guarantee we miss
A meeting with this well-groomed friend – whom we gush forward to kiss!

The other thing that takes our time are shelves which will have changed,
From things stocked there just yesterday for a whole new different range!
    They then held sauces, pickles, herbs, now they are cereals, flour,
It seems they shift the goods around almost by the hour!

Another moan I feel is just, are aisles which become blocked,
Not only by us gossipers, but with goods when shelves are stocked.
    To remedy this problem I suggest aisles are one way,
With fines for those who break the rules, which they are made to pay!

The shopping trolley waywardness I have not mastered yet,
It still continues where it will however mad I get!
    Strangely and quite annoyingly my toddlers managed to
Get it to go the way they wished, and do what they said to do!

A long time at the checkout is the final breaking straw
Though I retain composure inside – I hate it all!
I do not blame the checkout girl – Lord knows, her task is great,
    Especially with folk like me whom shopping does frustrate!

But supermarkets are now with us, and they are here to stay
To be always there when needed, open for trade each day.
    So next time that I do my list, more time will then ensure
A chance to relish extra 'treats' which I so much deplore!

Money

In a future life, should I return to dwell upon this earth,
I'll come as something needed, a thing of personal worth!
   I thought I might be jewellery, a bracelet, or a ring,
But now I've chosen money which will buy most anything!

   As an important part of currency I would travel round a bit,
I would hide in many pockets, and on many tables sit.
   I'd go in cars, on trains, in planes, the world I would explore,
Folk would be glad to see me – never me they would ignore!

   The breadth of all society would always welcome me,
I would be in closest contact so never lonely be.
   I'd mix with poor, and with élite who know what they are worth,
It would be good to be so close to those of noble birth!

   If I came as a humble coin I would mix with many folk,
But I would be more popular with those near stony-broke!
   I would be a part of a society both modest and élite,
So handy for a meter, or perhaps some nicer treat.

   If I came as a paper note say a tenner or a fiver
I'd be valued for my spending worth as a useful old survivor!
   If I could choose my spending role I would opt for films or shows,
For where an owner visits I am always known to go!

   I understand that the need to eat means I'll likely go on food,
Although tills in supermarkets is not really where I'd choose!
   In preference I'd be spent on fun, or investment in the bank
Where I would meet my friends again, be they Jean, Joan, Paul or Frank!

   If as a fifty note I came, there would be chance for me
To move within those circles where I think I ought to be!
   The poorer folk would not be there, so I'd mix within a class
Of those lucky ones who socialize to make their leisure pass!

This society of plenty uses wallets large and fat
Which occupy the pockets of suits not bought from rack.
    To be carried by a man with style who knows who's who, what's what,
Would please me so immensely that I'd excuse his bald and fat!

As a note which is expensive I'd stay cleaner than a fiver
Which is splashed round so readily as an everyday survivor!
    As a crisp fifty I'd circulate for quite some lengthy time,
Yes! to move in higher circles would suit my style just fine!

A credit card, modern and smart, I did consider but discard
Because their pressured and high-powered life is thought to be too hard!
    When a credit card is in his owner's grip he will get no peace at all,
He's used for all occasions – and constantly on call!

A card's handling is quite shameful (that swiping is so harsh),
Those card machines look very grim – they give a dreadful time to cards!
    The times I've witnessed them abused when they are near their end,
Is not the kindest humane way to treat a loyal friend!

I did consider a cheque book, once definitely 'a must',
But cards have become popular, so now people are not fussed!
    Cheques have an older image, slow, fiddly, undermined,
And their backing up by cheque cards is hurtful and unkind!

I admit that cards are treasured, kept near so not to stray.
Kept close in body contact through each and every day.
    But if he tries to escape his grind, his capture reaches such heights,
Informing banks, and also police – then he loses all his rights!

You know this money swapping is a fearful tiring drain,
For whatever currency I choose will go against the grain!
    So the decision I have made at last is to abandon all this scene
And return to earth as a peacock, so I only need to preen!

Gloucestershire Quirks

For those born here in Gloucestershire, some words we use are strange,
    They pepper conversations, in variety and range.
They enlarge on what we're saying, bring charm to mundane speech,
    They are individual parts of us, born with, and never teached!

When I was bathed I was told when young to wipe my body dry,
    Damp bodies make us 'spreedy', and this could make me cry.
When I had cuts on fingers, they were 'chaps' which hurt and split,
    Snowfire was used to better them – when it was heated up a bit!

Whenever I was out on walks I 'scuppied down' to wee
    To keep my bottom off the damp, behind a bush or tree!
Cold stones, Dad said, caused piles so sore I better had take care
    To always be most careful to protect those regions there!

To run and skip, play hopscotch, I wore 'daps' of canvas black,
    A word not in the dictionary available to track!
No mention of sugared 'dunkies', or 'lardies', that fatty cake,
    Or 'boughten' purchased from the shop, as a change from Mother's bake!

When hungry, 'nobbies' were so good (they are the bread's end crusts),
    Home after school, eaten with jam, for me they were a must!
Also Dad's scallops (spuds, battered and fried) a tasty filling tea,
    With brown sauce and some bacon – there could nothing nicer be!

When the coal fire died, refused to burn, the 'pilot' was put up.
    It drew the flame from down below to crackle, flare and gush!
When we were good last thing at night, an iron poker red
    Was plunged into some Tizer pop, for a treat before our bed!

We children said 'our Mother', 'our Dawn', 'our Gran,' 'our Gramp,' 'our' Dad.
    'Our Mother' tried to stop us – she thought it sounded 'bad'!
Elocution did not stop this trend, to make us more 'correct',
    Or Queen's English cause us to wish to change our dialect!

I'd like to think these things live on to be practised once again,
    That fires still blaze, and dialects live, and fatty foods remain.
That people will identify with things been said and done
    Which made our days, not long ago, a time of joy and fun!

Hilda

At Potgaston Farm, Hilda Peglar, from the age of four
    Helped her father on the farm, cleaning the yard and more.
She helped her mother in the house, in chores plenty, diverse
    And looked upon the bright side, when things could have seemed worse!

At twelve years old she helped with milking, when her brother Fred
    Went down with dreaded measles, so had to stay in bed.
By the light of a hung lantern, which they both did share,
    Hilda, beside Father, milked six cows herself out there!

She also, and quite regularly, fed chickens, calves, mucked pens,
    Picked stones up in the meadow, made the animals her friends.
Noted numbers, letters on the churns, before Cadbury's arrived
    To fetch the morning's milking, through lanes not very wide.

At home she scrubbed the toilet out – but did not have to empty!
    She cut newspaper into squares, to ensure supplies in plenty.
Candles removed, cleaned the holders, set matches close near by,
    For Father to do the lighting – small Hilda must not try!

Mother she helped with washing – farm things are very mucky!
    Scrubbed Father's smocks over a stool when they were very grubby!
    On Sundays watched the dinner until her parents did return
From their regular Sunday worship, then the children had their turn!

In the evenings she washed dishes, peeled potatoes, fetched in coal,
    Practised the piano after, sometimes with Father in duo.
Father liked all the good old hymns, 'Hil, let's have that last once more',
    So over it was once again, before her bed to Hilda called!

In service at just fourteen she went to Slimbridge Rectory,
    Away from home she was homesick for the farm and all her family.
At Hammond Farm, as a gift, she gained a lamb she loved so well,
    Who followed her on little walks – and whom she christened Mary Bell!

Tasks here were kitchen boiler, and also sitting-room grate,
    Then out to see to chickens, and also feed the drakes.
But at Backwell House, where prayers at nine saw a staff of some fourteen,
    Hilda helped at many jobs as a part of a large team!

At home she picked the apples for the farm cider that they made,
    Which was given to the Cadbury's men who for the shooting came!
At Christmas time the Factory to Mother Peglar did present
    An enormous box of chocolates for milk so regularly sent!

Hilda sums up her childhood life as 'Busy with lots to do'!
    She did not have much time to spare, with work to be got through.
But the good times balanced the heartache times, (like when lambs left on
                                                      market day),
    Says Hilda, 'We didn't have a lot, but we were happy in our way!'

My Friend

My friend I like to visit lives not many miles from here,
In a village in the Cotswold hills, which to him is very dear.
He was not born there, but in Stroud where he went to school and work,
    Where the pranks he played, with friends he'd made, was a daily fun-time quirk!
The old-style Gloucestershire he loves, especially its brogue,
He speaks it to me often, then he translates what he's told.
It can be broad, and it can be from quite another place,
    That it could die, and be all gone, he feels a big disgrace!
    My friend's never left this area and does not want to now,
He's a real old-fashioned countryman who grew up with horse and plough.

He now finds it hard to get about – but it hasn't stopped his tongue!
His legs may not behave themselves but his heart is very young!
His eyes light up when we reminisce and about his youth we talk,
    Before modern things took over, when people used to walk.
When Sunday was a relished day for those home free from work,
And a half-day on a Saturday regarded as a perk!
When things were much more simple, like sawdust on butcher's floor
    That was swept up very regularly, then replenished with some more.
    When deliveries were done daily, by bicycle from door to door,
Or in Ford vans, and with milk cans, to both rich and very poor!

Then men donned trilbies, women wore hats – there were best clothes on a
    Sunday.
People sang and whistled tunes – ate a fried breakfast, their mainstay!
Church bells rang, and people went – not always willingly it's true,
    And children did not have very much, but they'd find something to do!
When Sunday School and daily school did incorporate the same lads
Who planned larks for all seven days which were not really bad.
Like at Sunday School when dragging time caused a gallery clock to be put on
    By this band of resentful children, who'd been sitting there too long!
        Teacher said, 'Doesn't time go by?' and the whole class answered 'Yes!'
As they rushed out very early to escape the spiritual stress!

The same good teacher thought strongly that a spiritual bonding could
Continue, if taught early, into a person's adulthood.
A chosen child bound the master's thumbs with cotton very light,
    Which he broke apart with gusto to prove some bonding could be slight!
One day one naughty pupil wrapped the cotton round so tight
That his thumbs were locked together, which made his theory watertight.
    No method seemed to budge it, so a boy to ease his plight
    Produced a knife to cut him free, to the class's great delight.
    It must be said their laughter did more for them that day
Than any amount of teaching, or rules set to obey!

Another time at daily school – at the Parliament School in Stroud,
Their beloved Friday cricket was abandoned through wet ground.
All there were disappointed, except for one bookworm
    Who never had liked any sport, which he avoided through the term.
That afternoon the master asked for an essay from his class
About the game of cricket, a foreboding hateful task!
No-one wished to do it, but they had to all the same,
    Even that clever bookworm – totally ignorant of the game!
    So it was a dreadful pity, when his essay it did say
R.S.P. on his clean white page – meaning simply Rain Stopped Play!

Later, when with workmates my friend helped catch a curd tart thief
With an act which could be painful, although no-one came to grief!
Some mustard was mixed within a tart designed to make mouths hot –
    So they might know who was the thief, and know who he was not!
A day went by and suddenly a tart it did remain
When the naughty tiresome tart thief, for some reason did refrain!
Not a word was said, but they all guessed who, because someone had a thirst
    Which was not very nice for him, but could have been much worse!
    But which also taught a lesson, and caused some hours of mirth
To those hardy bunch of youngsters who had lived in Stroud since birth.

(Continued overleaf)

Upon the farm my friend worked hard – he began at 5am.
He worked all week, but he loved his work, and he'd do it all again!
Before, he'd worked as a butcher's boy, but dead things were not his scene,
    Farm life was vibrant and alive, near to his veterinary dream.
His dog, Jacco, his loyal friend, was his close companion,
Who guarded all upon the farm and ensured the work was done.
But Jacco had an unusual quirk when people he admitted
    Could only leave farm premises when Jacco them permitted!
This was a scourge for courting folk, when their secret lover hide
Was impossible for them to leave until dog Jacco did decide!

I could go on but I must stop, though I know there will be more
Of these lovely little memories which from my dear friend pour!

My Forgetfulness

I am getting most forgetful; I leave reminders around the place
'Cos I'm geared up to remembering so I will not lose face.
I've tried things to remind me – labels, cards, lists, empty pots,
    To assist me through their presence
                to remember things forgot!
I remember best when in the night my mind should shut down tight
When things are jotted blindly down regardless of no light.
But in the morn what I have writ is just a messy scrawl
    Which no-one can decipher – so why write things down at all?

Did I say I'm more forgetful – I don't think I said before,
That I have funny habits, like notes on toilet doors!
Labels stuck onto telephones, bits scattered up the stair,
    And a cardboard box in the doorway –
              to remind me it is there!
The T.V and computer have stickers on their screens,
Which means no-one can view a thing until the message there is seen!
Things hung on knobs, on beds, on chairs to nudge and give a clue
    Of what I wish to remember, and what I have to do!

Quite childishly I've scrawled on wrists and up along my arm.
Tied knots in things, then prompt forgot – which later caused alarm!
Stuffed notes down my front, where they stayed to remain decent,
    And in pockets of coats where masses of notes,
              Needs a memory to know which is recent!
I'm sorry for not writing earlier but I'm forgetful now you know,
I knew I must answer a letter, then I remembered to you it was owed.
That shelf as you know, is the first place I go, when I remember
I need a reminder,
    So as to how I forgot is a bit of a shock, but a note will remind for
                              December!

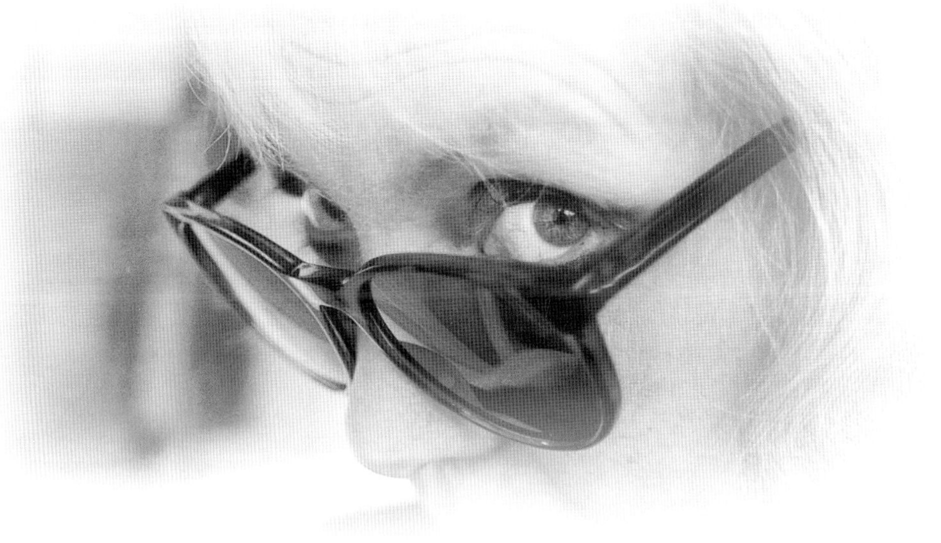

Pursuits

You'll find the following section is about the things we do
At work, at home, at pleasure - and their effect on me and you!
It seems, in almost anything, hazards will lie in store,
So these poems may convince you nothing's simple anymore!

Once the environmental closeness of garden, home or bed,
Offered tranquil security - or so we have been led!
But now it's shown they harbour things which are not very nice,
To confront with trepidation - or avoid at any price!

Those pleasures which once glossed our day are dulled for various reasons,
As we strictly discipline ourselves to self-imposed restrictions!
We give up biscuits, buns, and sweets - butter went long ago!
These things, they say are bad for us - not good for us to know!

Once holidays were few and prized - the excuse for some excess,
People met, ate, and had their fun, and wore their Sunday dress.
They engaged in simple pleasures, made enjoyments of their own,
So different from us modern throng, who have it all - yet moan!

I've discovered that the best pursuits are those gone by and over.
Past ones that I can think about with a subtle hint of clover!
In memories, bad things do not hurt, all people there are kind,
Cold days are warm, and mild days hot, and we take things as we find!

In reality, we know quite well, things were not quite like that.
There were bad days, with feelings hurt, but these swiftly we've forgot
So that within our minds we can create the paradise we crave,
As we elaborate, and contemplate those memories we have saved.

I am a Water Diviner

I am a water diviner, yes, I really can divine,
    I managed it just yesterday and now I do it fine.
I once thought it a load of rot, magic and just not true
    But now that I can do it, I no longer hold that view.

The claim that water under the ground was detected from above
    Appeared to me ridiculous and worthy of a snub.
But now I'm a Diviner and this water comprehend
    I take back the opinion it was all some great pretend!

In my first try at divining it was two bent wires I used,
    Which were held above our septic tank, but this my wires confused.
You see water must be running, or at least be on the go,
    So I should have pulled the flush a bit to make the liquid flow!

My try above the water pipe was my triumph of success
    Water I knew already there, but the thrill was none the less!
I held my wires quite loose and still as I walked along the road,
    Until suddenly they crossed and pulled, without them being told!

In another spot it happened too where no water there should be,
    That suddenly was a worry, 'cos it meant a leak to me.
If this was so, I clearly saw things there were not quite right,
    The thought of floods and water cost caused worry through the night.

Why did I learn divining and water deep down seek?
    Why cause myself this misery when before I lived in peace?
Tell me who needs diviners when water pipes are everywhere
    Which spurt water the moment a hole is dug somewhere!

But I still am a Diviner 'cos I proved it yesterday,
    And I'm endowed with this special gift which I can, if asked, display!
While I do not fully understand how the whole thing operates,
    I feel that's not important, because I can divine, for heaven's sake!

No Pleasure in Things Anymore

There's no pleasure in things anymore,
The enjoyment of good things in store.
Whenever we sample pursuits once so simple,
We're lectured by some health-freak bore.
Food once a delectable pleasure,
Eaten freely by all without measure,
Experts now imply, we exclude, lest we die
Of those cholesterol foods we all treasure!

        Once relaxing was thought to be good,
        So we sat and digested our food.
        But now it seems right that our flab we must fight,
        So we get up whatever our mood.
        This applies with our holidays too,
        No bare skin or sunbathing for you!
        Those rays will cause harm – not add to your charm,
        'So keep in the shade, dear, please do!'

Attachments of amorous kinds,
Are best kept within wishful minds.
With new risks in store we dare hardly do more,
'Keep your hands to yourself, do you mind!'
Most folk like a wee drink or two,
To lift spirits up when they're blue.
But a recent reminder says to stop would be kinder –
Or drink a less potent brew!

Fast driving was passion and fun
As men on M1 raced the ton!
But today's traffic clogging, means it's faster when jogging,
So motors stay home while they run.
Not changed is the attitude to work,
When to toil is still right – not to shirk!
They claim efforts we make, will benefit our heart rate,
The money, of course, is a perk!

        So with pleasures gone and depleted,
        It leaves us all somewhat deflated
        As we wonder what's left which won't have us bereft,
        So we can once again be elated.
        If people had sense they'd rebel,
        Say 'We've only one life. What the hell!
        'Let's enjoy what we have, and indulge in all bad
        And in everything not advocated!'

The Common Cold

Usually in winter, people get the common cold,
'Common', when for all ages, young, middle-aged, or old!
'Common', when noses which choose to run are gently blown and wiped,
And common to upgrade to flu –
        a sort of status hype!

The common cold is versatile – it gets us out of things,
It stops us going into work or visiting boring things!
It is handy when it's catching, 'Please do not get too near!'
It is handy to procure a cold –
        because a cold's a thing to fear!

A cold outweighs its drawbacks, 'They go quicker when in bed!'
It's an excuse for doing nothing, 'Oh darling, my poor head!'
When things go wrong it lets you off, 'This cold has fuzzed my brain!'
And no-one wants you cooking –
        when you just might sneeze again!

Colds come in many kinds, who knows which one is yours?
People will not investigate because germs breed fast indoors!
A husky phone call will inform a cold is safe with you,
Then you decide the type, extent –
        walking-wounded, or the flu!

I know I sound hard-hearted to observe colds in this way,
And I know they make us miserable - plague for ages, or a day.
We can feel quite poorly, our eyes run and we get hot,
But it must be said, when we're tucked in bed –
        who can tell how ill or not?

Back pain is a comparison - the scourge of industry!
'My back's done in!' someone will say, 'It's to the surgery'!
There the doctor pulls and pushes, to gauge extent of plight,
Then he writes out a prescription -
                of full rest for a fortnight!

Our ownership of the common cold will only last so long,
Which is so different from 'a back' which can go on, and on, and on!
For my own choice I will take the cold, though it could turn into flu
It really all depends you see -
                on what I've planned to do!

The Bed

Of all the contents in your home, your bed will know you best,
It feels when you are wide awake, when you require some rest.
It anticipates your troubles, when life has made you glad,
    It rejoices when you're happy, it welcomes when you're sad!

When you lie upon its surface you become bonded as one,
It accommodates your body shape – head, arms, legs or tum!
It gets to know your personal smell, and the warmth which you will bring,
    It waits patiently all day for you – ready to let you in!

Your bed sees you at your very worst, it admires you at your best!
It knows if you've been out late, or in early for a rest.
When you are feeling worried – or happy in yourself,
    It knows of precious moments which it keeps all to itself!

Tell me, who feels and sees you the moment you arise?
Who awaits you when you are so tired, can scarce keep open eyes?
Does your bed complain when you are ill, or sick upon its cover?
    No! it just hangs on, amid the pong, wishing it will soon be over!

Yes! your bed is so adaptable, it is there for all your life.
It's there when you are newly born, and when you are a child.
It's there when as a teenager you loll in it all day;
    It's shared when you're an adult. When old, a strong mainstay!

Beds can contain some drawbacks, but they are very few
In years gone by they harboured bugs which sucked the blood from you!
A sore or two they can produce if lain in for a while,
    And the bed-bound might resent them when their constant presence riles!

Beds give the added service of versatility through our lives
When there to take in frightened babes, and cuddle up to wives.
To sit upon, and read in, lull children off to sleep,
    Drink tea in, watch T.V in, or talk, dream, think, or weep!

So thank you to my dear divan, can you hear me way up there?
A few hours yet and I'll be up to receive your loving care.
Tomorrow you shall have a treat, I will stay all day with you,
    As a token of appreciation for someone who is true!

The Hot-Water Bottle

How we treat our hotties is shameless to behold;
We hug them close when they are hot, and discard them when they're cold!
We cherish them when they are new, wrap them in jackets trim,
But when they're old and leaky – just throw them in the bin!

Few other items on this earth are treated quite this way –
Except some aged spouses when they have seen their day!
A bottle's life is intimate, it's close cuddled every night,
Some folk prefer their bottle – before husband or wife!

Another sadness as nights warm, is their abandonment in Spring,
Just think you have been close for months, now you ignore the poor old thing!
Sad Hottie is just pushed away on dark shelf or on hook,
He is not wanted, seen, or touched – a sleeping partner, sad, forsook!

A cruel problem and quite unfair is when he has a leak,
Often it is not him to blame, it's his stopper which has seeped!
Now when no stopper can be found to fit his poor old neck,
No-one can use him anymore – so he's condemned as an old wreck!

His faithful service over years is abandoned suddenly,
As we awake all wet and cold and as grim as we can be!
We leap out quick with wicked words, so harsh, and cruel, unkind,
To change our clothes, and sheets, and things, while poor Hottie lies and pines.

We all know that when we age such mistakes like this occur,
But humans are not thrown away for a new dry him or her!
Instead we cherish those we've loved and ease their personal plight,
So they will be more confident during the following night!

In a lifetime cuddling bottles I've tried a brand or two.
I had a stone one when quite young – there was a tin one too!
The stone one it was firm, smooth glazed – ridged, dented was the tin,
All well wrapped up in blanket so as not burn my skin!

My bottle I still love a lot despite a hot husband,
To clasp Hottie to my tummy and press him with my hand.
He's cuddled tight up to my chest, or back as I get older,
But I confess as he gets cold, I give him the cold shoulder!

The Telephone Directory

The telephone directory can make everyone a star,
'Phone possessors are all listed – you just look and there you are!
It's an open book for all the world to gauge what we're about.
    If we're rich or poor or something more, it might just help us out!

The Directory gives information in area and name,
It reveals those little details which could make possible our fame.
It shows if you're plain So-and-So, a Dr, Rev. or Prof,
    Or if you're a Sir Robert, to whom in past times we all doffed !

The way you are presented could shape your life for you,
Perhaps indicate your politics, red, yellow, green or blue.
Maybe hint about your income, house owner with a car,
    To indicate the person that you'd like to think you are!

Just stop and think of BARRATT-RHYS-PHELPS: he might be someone
                                                           to know!
With wealth to us quite daunting, his abode could tell us so.
Does he reside in The Old Dower House? No Road or Street for him,
    It sounds he's one of the upper crust, public school, that sort of thing!

Do you think a double-barrelled name can allow us more acclaim?
Diminish all the rest of us blessed just with single names?
Are SMITH or THACKER lesser folk, and viewed as second rate?
    Society appears to think we are – but we'll investigate!

Imagine an address which has a Road or Street,
It may not sound interesting – with no members of élite!
The area description might indicate that there
    Are ordinary, worthy people, but perhaps with not much flair!

Now let us place them somewhere, like an Avenue, Grove or Square,
Our view of them might change a bit – to people who head somewhere!
Doubtless they'll own their thirties house, have family at boarding school,
    A double garage on their drive, and perhaps an ornate pool!

If they lived in Flats, they'd park out in the street,
If in a Terrace in the town, a car might be a treat!
If in a Lane – well that is hard, they could be anyone
    In finance, or in chicken feed – more detail could help this one!

An address without a number may lift folk socially,
Just to have a name, it's said, will hint individuality!
A lone house name could shout to all, 'I'm not estate, or Row!
    I'm exclusive and quite special – this name will show you so!'

If they were Profs they might reside in a nice Parade,
With a basement, curving stair, lodgers of upper grade.
A study lined with panelled oak and a courtyard, where they could
    In summer entertain their chums with fine wine and good food!

As Earls or Dukes, they might boast a gorgeous Country Pile
And an estate within the country of some square hundred miles!
Display a list of entries, so their large-scale management
    Would communicate efficiently in business matters of extent!

The listed Business numbers are always happy to oblige,
To discuss with us a business deal for things they can provide.
Some have just lines, some use a box, some opt for bold and black,
    But they all ensure their names are there so finances stay on track!

Some names reflect, incredibly, the work folk undertake,
Like GARDENERS who work in Gardening, BAKERS who really bake!
A GAUGE who makes Thermometers, a BELLING in alarms,
    A CARPENTER in Timber, and a FARMER who owns a farm!

The telephone directory could be studied in our schools
So future populations will not be social fools.
But would an insight through this book allow them to unfurl
    A correct assessment of the social life in their own corner of the world

(A fictional directory, and tongue-in-cheek observation of the dangers of stereotyping.)

All Wrapped Up

Everything comes wrapped today, nothing is ever bare.
We have to wrench packaging away to get to what's in there!
Sometimes it's shrouded – hidden deep – in polyester chips,
    At other times it shows its all, sharp shapes and curvy bits!

To break through all this armoury takes strength, which can quite daunt
When what appears an easy task is not simple as first thought!
Admittedly a thumb and nail are adequate for some,
    But a full toolkit is maybe used before the job is done!

We expect that cardboard boxes will need a prise or two,
So we're equipped with knives and wrenches, to pierce and slice them
        through.
We might employ some pliers, snips, for staples, metal bands,
    For we expect a good strong box will need more than just bare hands!

The plastic world around us has infiltrated Goods,
It is seen on household fittings, and on every kind of food.
It is seen on things which once were loose – and better for all that,
    And humans also do it! Do you own a plastic mac?

Yes, most every food is tight-wrapped in plastic of some kind,
Which mostly is not needed, it is a fearful bind!
Once it was nice to feel our buys to see if they were sound,
    We accepted germy atmospheres – and that goods fell on the ground!

When vegetables are all wrapped up they go mouldy from within,
They try to breathe, but instead grow pale within their tight film skin!
When unadorned in paper bags, panic sweating was unknown -
    When outside and quite dirty, they felt they were at home!

It is plain absurd to wrap up swedes – their life is down in muck!
Its mad to push poor cucumbers within a plastic sock!
Lettuce and green things like the air – they hate imprisonment,
    In cellophane they wilt and slime in unhappy discontent!

At least oranges and bananas have escaped this wrapping fate,
Things which have peel don't need all that – they're wrapped in natural state!
Their natural wrapping is the best because it rots away, is gone,
    Unlike the plastic variety, which lives on and on and on!

However, understandably, fish and meat will stain,
And there is sense in wrapping things, when a wrapping bears a name.
I know packs are much easier to pick up when in a rush,
    But I would not like their bound-up state – restricted, gagged
        and trussed!

In the case of household appliances, some are much better wrapped,
To secure them, when in transit, from the risk of being scratched!
I think so, too, of other things, like mirrors, glass and saws,
    They're a danger not just to themselves but also to us all!

Do you remember those loose biscuits all muddled in the box?
Sultanas in their sacking which we ate unwashed as snacks?
Cheese dry with rind that we could taste, which the grocer sliced with wires,
    It is sad, progress and wrapping has made all that expire!

The Crazy World of Up and Down

The world is such a funny place,
    we're either up,
    or down.
We're either high up in the clouds,
    or in the dumps,
    let down!
When down on luck, down in the world,
    downhearted,
    down the pit!
When things look up, up in the air,
    we're uplifted
    in our spirits!

When we are down we degrade ourselves,
    go down
    in estimate!
When we are up, we uphold ourselves,
    feel we are
    upper rate!
When down-trodden, and down-and-outs,
    then we are
    down-at-heel
With hand-me-downs from the upper crust,
    who know not
    how downcasts feel!

Up-market clothes are worn uptown,
        with hair
        which is upswept!
Upgraded restaurants feed the upper class,
        those of the
        upper set!
A deposit put down, will secure for us
        house, car,
        holiday,
And should we go Down Under,
        we'd fly up high
        for all that way!

So we will not at all be down,
        uplifted
        we will be,
And take a walk down to the pub,
        or drink up
        a cup of tea!
We will sit down to down our drink,
        and when it has
        slid down,
We'll then all be uplifted –
        which will suit all
        down to the ground!

The Garden

Our garden we are led to think is a haven safe and calm
Despite those vicious plants within waiting to do you harm.
    They lurk there very prettily to tempt you to come by,
Then lash out with their spikes and thorns to catch you in the eye!

We cannot move for all their ploys, so artful and so cute,
Fruit trees designed to break a bone just climbing for their fruit!
    To pick a rose you risk great pain as it spikes you in the thumb,
And should it miss this easy chance – then it'll get you in the bum!

The scent they give is lethal – don't ever try a whiff,
You'll find a sneeze, a wheeze, a choke, can be triggered with a sniff!
    Oft times a tender stroke or touch will a raise a rash so sore
That will irritate for days, or weeks, some months, or even more!

Grasses they can look lovely as they wave within the breeze,
They do not sting, cause us to itch, or cause us much to sneeze.
    But should you try to pick a leaf of some great big showy type,
It'll cut your finger to the bone as good as any knife!

I think the bees who visit plants are fellows brave indeed,
Though they do it for necessity and for their daily needs.
    If I should have to do the same I'd wear a safety hat,
My bare head would not venture there – I've got more sense than that!

I now know why those garden pests eat all our cabbage plants,
I'd do the same if I like them was allowed the slightest chance!
    I bet each nibble they pursue is to settle some dispute,
For minor quarrel, just a leaf – an outright war the root!

It's obvious the birds around hate everything below,
The pigeons peck the tender plants, and most anything which grows!
    The other birds seize berries, fruit, and then what do they do?
They spit the stones to show disgust, and mess on all heads in view!

The way I think to solve this dread is to get rid of the lot.
To cut and scrape, level and burn, then concrete the whole plot.
    Then I could roam, and sit, and snooze and be completely free
Of those conniving, cruel plants who daily torment me!

House Plants

The houseplants that are in my house can live a life of utter hell
    When neglected and forgotten, or they're treated very well!
They are watered so they almost drown, then thirst when parched and dry,
    From one day to another they could live or they could die!
They suffer pressure daily – 'Will I be kept or thrown away,
Will I be put in scorching sun, or hid from the light of day?
If on stairs I do reside, can I risk those pounding feet?
    Or if by blistering heaters, will I wither in the heat?'

Very frequently mine are fed too much, or given none at all!
    Dumb house-plants cannot speak or cry, beckon, or shout or call!
They cannot use large, tearful eyes to question, beg, or plead,
    So they receive much when not wanted, or nothing when in need!
Some either sweat in tiny pots, or drown in vessels vast,
When at the sign of illness they are hauled out and recast!
Some stand up well to all this change, some feel the space too great,
    So they wilt and droop, go pale and stoop, and die at a fast rate!

The worst part for any potted plant is expulsion to the cold,
    Which can occur when they are ill or when they're growing old.
Without a qualm they are thrust outside in ice, and rain, and snow
    Because when a plant is over, it simply has to go!
The best plants to survive the strain are those which do not flower.
Not for them bright blooms to show off, for all eyes to devour!
Instead they boast a foliage, glossy and ever dense,
    Until a leaf curls up and browns, then gone is their defence!

My house-plants, I am sad to say, have a short and tenuous life.
    In summary, their life is praise followed by strain and strife!
It seems the general rule for plants for those who say they care,
    Is to worship them 'til the flowers die, then throw them out somewhere!
More fortunate are the outdoor plants, at least their roots can touch
To comfort and console them, when they are hacked too much!
To nurture a brotherly spirit not allowed for plants inside,
    Where, at their owner's mercy, they struggle to survive!

Cars

Can a car resemble a human as a man sometimes his pet?
Can the petrol that they guzzle, compare with human blood so red?
Are their engines their nerve system, as I have within me?
Do they have off-days as we do, when they're right old miseries?

    If a car is like it a human, how do I fit this mould?
    Do I look like just like my Subaru – nice when new, but getting old?
    Have I lost a little colour, that youthful pristine glow?
    Well, if all of that is really true, then I don't wish to know!

I confess we match in some small ways, I jump when I am cold!
I am grumpy when my temperature drops, when warm I'm good as gold!
I am a little rusty, should in bodywork invest,
So that after a overhaul I would sail right through my test!

    Quite exceptionally our temperaments are wonderfully matched,
    Neither get excited nor drive around roads fast.
    We are not like presumptuous steeds who hurtle in lane three,
    We are not champagne guzzlers – we're more a cup of tea!

But there are a few cars I know who'll not from boyhood leave,
Just like their ageing owners, their boy-racer instincts still they heed.
And while they have seen better days, their engine says they've not,
So they roar and race around the place – as bits fall off and rot!

A car that is quite close to me is just as I've described,
He is quite old and dented now, but he boasts a four-wheel drive!
While it looks as if he's lived his last, he tries hard to deceive
As he roars and revs, just to stretch his legs, every morning as he leaves!

Cars most compare with humans when they can be replaced –
Should they fail to function correctly, there's plenty more will suit your taste!
Some might choose one who's second-hand, been round the lanes a bit,
Or a new young one, suave, and so strong, on whose seat you're first to sit!

But please do not make the sad mistake of keeping the old wreck,
If he's old and slow, he deserves to go, he will cost to keep in check!
You'll be better off get rid of him to that scrapyard in the sky
So that any of his functioning bits can be used before he dies!

Super Hints

I have a little book here, which shows the easy way
Of doing almost anything which arises through the day.
It uses things which commonly lie idly around,
Such as ammonia, whiting, borax, gin,
and an oxalic acid compound!

Armed with my book, I can easily have a home that sparkles bright,
Without the need for fancy sprays to remedy my plight.
My book tells me just what to do to ease the cleaning pain
Of scrubbing, rubbing, scraping, spraying –
so my energy's contained!

Should my wood floor get a stain or two, it can be bleached with
lemon juice!
Should the drain cover get slimy, a bonfire is of use!
If my carpet's singed by some wayward spark, try a potato rub,
Lime deposits on the bath and loo
need acid and rubber gloves!

Washing soda will make sinks fresh, neat bleach on fungus walls.
Boiled vinegar for kettle scale, linseed for wooden floors.
Our platinum, gold, diamonds and pearls, ammonia will clean –
And also all those other gems
that we own and with which we preen!

In Food it says cool vinegar for pickled onions crisp!
Tender young shoots of nettles will taste like fresh spinach!
When you have killed your chicken, you should pluck it while it's warm,
And eating is the best test
to see if oysters do you harm!

Broth clarified for aspic should be chilled and the fat removed.
Hot toast with roast beef dripping is most definitely approved.
Your Easter Eggs can be coloured should you bind with onion skin,
If your fizzy drink is tired and flat –
just pop some bicarb in!

When cleaning up your best mink coat please don't use starch or bran,
The female mink is sensitive, these old methods are too strong!
Small stains are removed easily with magnesium carbonate,
And silk used for fur storage –
when it's time they 'hibernate'!

In the section about the body, bad breath is simply cured
By chewing fresh cardamom seeds, or some lemon if endured!
Rose, spices and some sherry will 'secure a breath of flowers',
But it's best to limit dosage –
or you'll be tipsy in an hour!

Liquid paraffin rubbed before a bath will keep a youthful skin;
Not asses' milk, as we all thought, to lie and wallow in!
For shiny hair the Victorians swore by a beaten egg or two,
I actually tried this method once –
but it could work well for you!

To revitalise our facial skin a face mask is required,
Once mud was used or crocodile dung but today these aren't advised!
Instead try fruit, oats, or herbs – they're nicer in their smell,
But it's nice to know that if we like –
we can use some dung as well!

(Continued overleaf)

Raw onion is for balding pates, and also coconut oil.
Mayonnaise for a hair conditioner – but not if rancid, rank or spoiled!
Blackheads and nasty open pores respond to steam and lemon juice,
But avoid spiced foods or alcohol –
or this treatment is no use!

The Miscellaneous section says you can budge decanter stoppers
With little taps around the neck, or their immersion in warm water!
An eiderdown will not slide or slip with strips of cloth sewn in,
And a loose broom handle
should be wet when it is hammered in.

Should high tea require butter balls, a meat hammer will mould those!
If you wish to syphon petrol, there's a safe way here disclosed!
For those who detest smokers, but do not wish to say,
The book says burning candles,
will take the smell away!

Yes, this book is full of good ideas, I read it all one night.
And I shall try some recipes to see they work all right.
I know that when I next have fleas I won't use paraffin,
Instead I'll drink dark whisky –
it's an antidote for everything!

(Inspired by Supertips: Over 500 Hints to Make Life Easy,
by Moyra Bremner.)

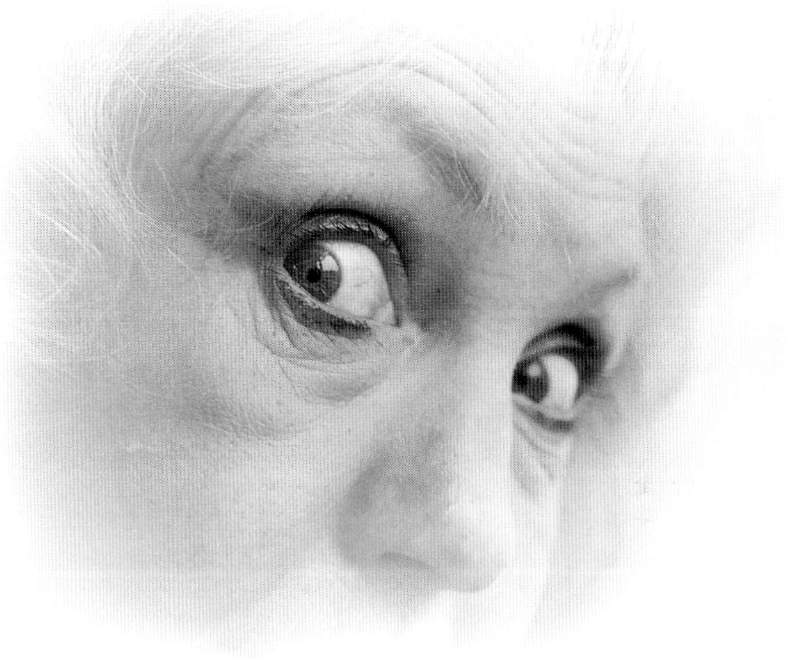

Body Parts

This section on our body parts shows the diversity
Of various bits, who wish to prove their individuality.
They here have proved that although they work within a team
They are not totally nameless, so they claim their self-esteem.

Some body parts are dowdy – these I've chosen to leave out –
Like arms and legs which wave and run, but have little else to flout!
The brain is left out also, that head man who runs the show,
'Cos we all know that without him other bits would just not go!

Of those gurgly parts down deep inside I will no mention make,
Except the heart, our most vital part, I feel he should partake!
Waists are not there either, because we see too much
Of them in glossy magazines, where they measure such and such!

Instead it is the smaller parts which have hidden depths not seen,
As they work away without display with little tendency to preen!
They do the most amazing work, without them we'd be lost,
Although some can be re-fit, and some I've heard are false!

These introduced new-comers need a period to conform,
When the home in which they're placed, is not the one where they were born!
A plastic bit might be a better bet than some secondhand has-been
Because he'll do what he is bid, and his youth will make him keen!

So this will be a tribute to what we are about,
Those varied bits within us which daily sort us out.
Their feelings and their functions, as they labour to attain
A life for their employer that is healthy, happy, sane!

A Mirror Never Lies

A mirror is a hateful thing, it shows up all our flaws,
It shows when we are tired and wan, as our wrinkles it explores!
It highlights all those lumpy bits with searching, probing eyes,
And informs we are not as we thought –
      because a mirror never lies!

This gazing at our outward self is a mesmerizing fault,
We know our mirror is not kind, but we're drawn there in revolt!
We twist about to see all sides, for a positive surprise,
But no matter how we pose, contort –
      we know a mirror never lies!

A more convenient hand mirror will view our sides and back,
Which we wish as slim and shapely – firm with nothing there too slack!
But our desires are rent and lost as we sadly realise
That bits stand proud where not allowed –
      in a mirror which never lies!

Dressed up on occasion, we decide we look just fine.
'Clothes maketh man', the saying saith, and we believe the silly line!
And even though a smart outfit can some bad bits disguise,
There is a limit to ingenuity –
      says a mirror which never lies!

But is this true I ask myself – are mirrors always right?
What of those Arcade mirrors which show us short or of great height!
Which say we are a matchstick, or wide with great big thighs,
You see, sayings are wrong after all –
      some mirrors can tell lies!

I shall buy a new one straightway to show me as I feel,
As sleek, well-groomed and confident, with oodles of appeal!
As a person with no spare bits – flawless, perfect and so wise,
Viewed honestly and kindly
      through a mirror which sometimes lies!

Hair

The body part most pampered is definitely our hair,
    Admired and preened, protected, with every single care.
Shampooed, and styled and nourished with products by the score,
    And when with age it gradually fades,
        then its colour is restored!

The reason for this slavery is because it is on top;
    So obvious for all to see, whether sleek or a wild mop!
It is a statement as to what we're like, it yells out 'This is me!'
    So we rinse and foam, spray, curl and comb,
        to be viewed as we would be!

Hairdressers through the ages have adapted to this trend,
And no longer scalp a vulnerable head when to their power it descends!
No longer do they cut all off – as with my pony tail,
    Which went like that, in a minute flat,
        as I let out a wail!

'Please shape it in the natural wave', Mother's message went,
The morn I most reluctantly was to the salon sent.
They cut and washed, and set me in the tightest curls yet pinned,
    So I caught the bus to the furthest stop
        and crossed the common in the wind!

When mother saw she was so cross, 'What's happened to your hair?
I was told they were reputable, but there's not much hair care there!
You look as if you have walked home through wind, and rain, and snow!'
    I kept it to myself I had –
        no need for her to know!

Gladly we are more casual now – no stiff bouffants and lotions,
No tight, tight perms, or stiff kiss-curls which have no sense of motion.
Instead we're loose, we're wild, we're free, so all the world can see
    That we're not as prim and proper
              as they make us out to be!

Our hair gives personality, and oozes sex appeal!
It rejuvenates our youthfulness as to how we used to feel!
It states if we're a dormouse or a lion who can roar
    And most obviously it shows to all
              what this person's aiming for!

Eyes

Eyes are so energetic, they never do stay still,
They're always busy seeing things, they never have their fill.
They dart about, and blink and wink, and look you in the eye,
They eye up people whom they like, and we wipe them when we cry!

Some eyes are brown, and some are blue, and some can be found green.
Others are clear, or bloodshot red, some somewhere in between!
Some eyes are opened, speaking volumes, their expression really talks,
Some are guarded, strained, tired, surprised – some stand out on their stalks!

We try to make them bigger by endowing them with paint,
With drops we make them clearer when we believe they ain't!
We wear our glasses so as to see those things we cannot see,
We see eye-to-eye with other folk, when with them we agree!

Unlike most other body parts, eyes never make a sound,
As they glance and peer, roll and hold fear, you cannot hear the ball go round!
It could be thought as years pass, worn parts might rub and grate –
But I'm assured, thank goodness, eyes do not get into that state!

TONGUES

From all our well-used body parts, our tongue is wagged the most
As it tastes, and swirls our food around, and helps it down the throat!
    It forms our words, and licks our stamps – it is coated when we're ill,
It is dry when we are frightened – and to hold it takes some skill!

Our tongues are pink, and moist and long, and fixed into our throats,
They bleed a lot should they be bit, or sore when we eat toast!
    When tender it is hard to speak, which seems to please the men,
But women recoup talking time, when they are healed again!

Without our tongue we all would grunt, and gesture with our hands!
Without a tongue we would not taste, food would appear quite bland.
    Without our tongues our lives would lack those senses which we love,
And people hate to lose their tongues and miss those things above!

In olden days tongues were ripped out – to torture and to punish,
Scolds wore an awesome metal gag clamped down to make them hush!
    You can today buy oxen tongues – removed of course when dead,
Which are soaked before you cook them, and then eaten between bread!

Tongues are so very modest, their work often unseen.
They rarely speak unless spoken with, they set no stylish scene!
    They've no pretence of prettiness, which teeth will oftimes seek
And I for one will not tie mine – as I like too much to speak!

Chests, Bosoms or Busts

The chest is sometimes called a chest - it's sometimes called a bust.
It sometimes called a bosom on the female sex of us!
    It is small when we are little, it expands as we get big,
To develop chests boys will work hard – girls do not do a fig!

Our chests are very prominent because of where they're placed
Up high where we can hug them, or when sitting to rest a plate!
    They can be quite a nuisance should they project too much,
And get in the way at work and play, so we harness them and such!

Jokes abound about our bosoms, how they can suffocate
Any insect that falls down there, and their low survival rate!
    When if bosoms are top-heavy we fall upon our face,
And they always march before us to come first at any race!

When people think theirs are too large and wish they were less ample
They starve and slim, or hold them in to create a smaller sample!
    Those who are small, will do anything at all, to create those extra pounds
So they exercise about, and pad themselves out, so to achieve more than
        small mounds!

I think, without our bosoms, fashion shops would go downhill,
There'd be a drop in purchases, and money in the till.
    For if we kept the same old size, and our bodies not re-shape,
There'd be no need for a larger size and measurements with tapes!

So we'll hang on to our bosoms – or see enterprise go bust!
We'll put up with what nature's brought and not be over-fussed.
It would be pretty boring to see us uniform,
And destroy those 'busty' silly jokes with which boys and girls are born!

The Heart

Our heart is at the heart of us, it beats without us knowing.
  We rarely listen to it thump, but we trust it is still going.
We'd know, I know, if it had stopped, but we won't consider that,
  Instead we'll love and cosset it, and cut down on our fat!

  The heart has tender notions, of romance, passion and pain.
It is depicted with an arrow, to prove the very same!
  On cards it's seen in velvet, often satin is employed
To show the tender feelings for a girl of a love-sick boy!

Roses are sometimes linked with hearts, men send them to their loves,
  Often they are accompanied by a card like that above.
When he gives a rose a man will gain some fond place in her heart,
  And a memory for ever of a romantic, loved sweetheart!

  Within the culinary gory bit, hearts can be stuffed and ate.
Not human hearts I haste to say, nor a beloved pet!
  Indulgers say they're tasty, with onions or with chives,
But I have no heart to try them – I'd think of them alive!

The last and most unselfish is the gift of someone's heart
  To some poor suffering, sickly soul who needs another start.
Such a splendid act is the ultimate, when a life it will enhance,
    And give to someone who is sick, another, golden chance!

The Stomach

Who would ever be a stomach, at the mercy of the whims
Of us people who devour an assortment of things!
Imagine the bombardment as this and that appears,
    Some of which is sensible,
      but some is simply queer!

A healthy, lively stomach will have the energy
To utilize his muscles extremely vigorously!
He will squeeze and squash, and push and pull, so all is well mixed in,
    Then drown it all in juices –
      so no-one knows what it has been!

A stomach is seen as happy when he speaks aloud for food,
Makes strange and funny noises, which can sometimes sound quite rude!
Gurgles and groans to give no peace until a dinner is in sight,
    Then he works away as said above,
      well into night!

An unhappy, poorly stomach will not want anything,
He will turn his gut at any food should his owner let some in!
Should this occur, then he will say, enough's 'Enough, that's that!'
    And rid it all up suddenly
      upon the dining mat!

So it is wise to heed those things your stomach says to you,
Not mix your drinks, or eat rich things, as you are prone to do!
Instead be wise, observe the signs, so your stomach won't rebel
    And cause you to spend churning hours
      in awful sickly hell!

Bottoms

Why is it that our bottoms are doomed to lifelong scorn?
Why are they mocked and laughed at from the moment they are born?
   Why is this vital part of us, this clever dextrous bit,
     Considered universally, the lowest form of body kit?
Why are slender waists superior, or hips which are so trim?
Firm bosoms, and those long, long legs – more so for being slim?
   Or flat, firm tums with no spare tyre, for which we sweat and strain?
     But not our humble bottom – this is treated with disdain!

We hardly see our bottoms – without mirrors likely not,
We can't sit and face it jowl to cheek to relish what we've got!
   To wonder at its clever style, so versatile and plump,
     For with no chance of facing it – it feels a large round lump!
Though we still tend and clothe it, despite it hid behind,
We pat it and we squeeze it, we try hard to be kind.
   We sit on it, and plump it down, and waddle it or wiggle,
     But we most of all make jokes of it, and use it for a giggle!

While other parts are pampered, bottoms get no such treat,
Our hands we cream, faces make-up, aches receive soothing heat!
   Necks are massaged to relieve their pain, muscles are firmed by weights,
     But there's nothing for poor bottom – he's just left to his fate!
In olden times, and modern too, sad bottoms bore the flack,
While brains and hands did all the crime, poor bums they got the whack!
   When mouths stayed tight, and feet ran free, they got the cruel thong,
     Which really was so wicked, when they had done no wrong!

Without our bums we would be lost – we could not walk or sit!
We would not function normally without its clever split!
   We would be straight, lie, hop or jump, we'd never ride a bike,
     We would be robbed of many things which we all doubtless like!
So I suggest a special day, to expose bum's worthiness.
A National Day which will expound the extent of his prowess!
   A feast wherein the fare should be legs, breast and shoulders roast
     But not the rump – no not this time – he's our superior host!

FEET

Our feet are not our prettiest part, low down there, far away,
With a burden they have all their lives – to carry us each day.
For this reason, logic dictates, they should be flat and strong,
    So to disperse the cursed weight of large bodies on them long!

Should feet decide to pack it in, and leave us for a rest,
We'd not be really legless 'cos our legs would stand the test.
But ankles are not really formed to move our bulk along,
    They are too round to hold their ground, and they would look all wrong!

Feet suffer too from nasty things, like corns, hard skin and chaps,
They smell bad when they're sweaty, if they are wearing daps!
To make them much more palatable, for those who stand nearby,
    It is best to cream and powder them, and wipe them very dry!

Toe nails are not the nicest things – they thicken with our age,
Get in-grown, yellowed, horny, they've little advantage.
We try our best to perk them up with varnish, pedicures,
    But completely hidden within a shoe is the best bet to be sure!

Feet should be treated better – without them we'd be lost
Not only in convenience, but also in the cost.
A false new pair of hand-made feet would set us back a sum –
They might well walk, and hold our bulk, but not be half the fun!

The Itch

A conspiracy within nature dictates itches can't be scratched
However long an arm is, or the length or width of back!
Any sharp keen nail which would ease it all will find it hard to win
The battle to reach that torment spot which lies just beneath the skin!

That back itch will, without a doubt, cause contortions, twists and groans,
As you endure your agony, amid curses, oohs and moans!
Then desperately you beg for help, from someone who is near,
To alleviate your torture and make the itching disappear!

Itches sometimes seek other parts which protocol doth say
Should not be scratched in public at any time of day!
Should in these regions an itch occur, a scratch you must refuse.
You see, itches come when we don't want and where we
would not choose!

Itches are a real torture under plasters and in dressings,
Where only a knitting needle our agony will lessen!
And also deep within our throat when silence is the code,
So we struggle hard to hold coughs back – then we
suddenly explode!

To rid an itch in private, and to satisfy at ease
Is a delightful occupation as we scratch just as we please!
But then often quite maddeningly that itch will stay away,
To return when we're in company – and torment us all the day!

Skin Cells

The fact that skins have numerous cells which die and flake away.
    Is not the nicest, kindest thought to contemplate today!
That we are dying from outside is dreadful to behold
    When we know from a brand-new babe we are becoming old!

From the moment we arrive on earth, cells carpet all the ground.
    We shed them as we move about, and they get thrashed around!
They could be salvaged, all mashed up, and recycled as new skin,
    But we just let them lie there and rot, then they're used to grow things in!

We are always walking on our cells – even in the snow,
    They lie in cracks in floorboards, and in the grass we weekly mow!
We leave a trail we cannot see to reveal our haunts and ways,
    For billions are scattered in just a few odd days!

Remember other things on earth will leave their own cells too,
    Can these compare with our cells, in texture, size and hue?
Are cells from insects, shiny, very sharp, and extra hard,
    And from reptiles, brown and mottled – or from elephants very
        large?

Do fish cells float on water, or sink in ocean deep?
    If the world was tarmacked, could cells be shovelled in a heap?
Do they crackle when we tread on them, do they survive upon our tongue?
    If they are always renewing, why aren't we always young?

I'm looking at my hands now – my cells are firmly stuck,
    They don't look as if they want to leave, elsewhere to try their luck!
I suppose those new ones underneath will rid them with a heave,
    Which can be quite sad really, when they do not want to leave!

The one way that we see our cells is when they obviously
    Lurk as dandruff on our scalp – not a tasteful thing to see!
No, we're not proud to see them there, so profuse and white,
    So we brush them away quite quickly, to get them out of sight!

Yet we should face up to losing things before our body dies,
    Which can be more disturbing when right before our eyes!
Daily we accept nails will break off, our teeth and hair will fall,
    So we should too be able, to accept our cell renewal?

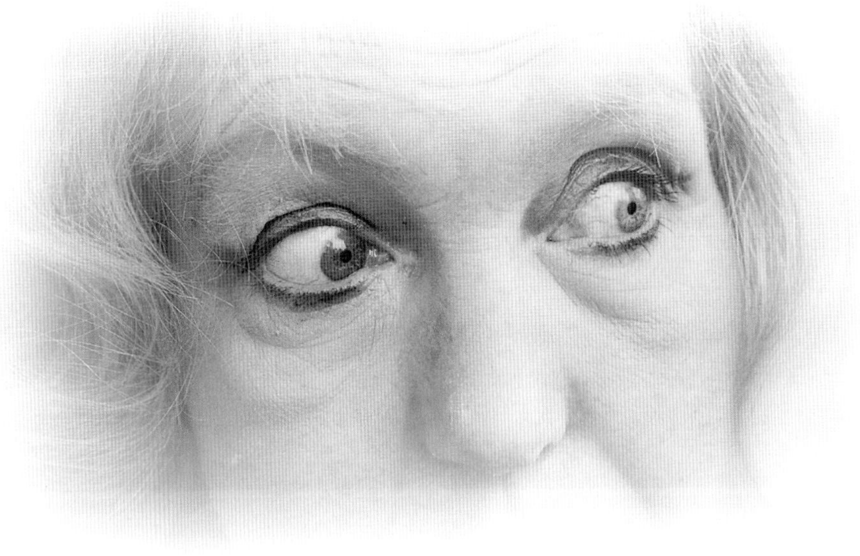

Livestock

The following rhymes on livestock are picked to make you see
The attributes and drawbacks of small creature company.
Not noted here those bulky blokes who do their power display,
But the minor, meeker, shyer chaps, who have not much to say!

We all know of those lofty ones such as elephants and bears,
Who speak not of their prowess when their size shows us they're there!
Those fearful limbs with muscles great, ooze an élitism not seen
Within those humbler, neater, breeds whom these larger ones demean!

The small ones to survive this trend require more character,
They cannot use a thwarting glance to make their wishes clear!
Instead they are more devious, when an intelligence profound
Allows them - although smaller - to ably stand their ground!

It is easier for those bulky chaps to live a good, long, life,
Their very size will help them should they be faced with strife!
The smaller, lesser, species face pain of death each day
At home, at work, within their bed, and even when at play!

Unfortunately for us humans, the smaller livestock often will
Because of their minuteness, with terror us instil!
Their quick movements, their stealthy steps, their ability to hide,
Can cause us all, both large and small, to churn away inside!

So there it lies before you of what you'll find in store,
An image of some creatures not considered much before.
There are of course so many more to include another time,
Should I think they are suitable to make into a rhyme!

The Invader

He menaced in the doorway, I backed up to the wall,
He took a step towards me, I could not move at all.
I edged up to the table, for a glass to strike him down,
    He had a light, quick, silent step –
        my heart began to pound!

He began to clamber on the bed – I screamed, 'Oh no! Get off!'
He took no notice of my pleas as my arms waved back and forth.
I tried to wrench away the sheet – to kick him to the floor,
    And when he stretched to touch my feet,
        I bolted for the door!

I slammed it tight – I knew quite well this would not stop the lout.
I'd met his family before, knew what they were about!
I'd found the only way to keep from their unwelcome charms,
    Was to keep them quiet within the room
        and set up an alarm!

But my shouting brought me no-one, I was alone with him!
I needed help from someone – but he would frighten all my kin!
No! I must sort him out myself, I had done so once before,
    So I strode right in, rammed down the glass –
        and pinned the spider to the floor!

Some cardboard held him safely, he was better at arm's length.
He sat and eyed me sadly, but I just felt contempt.
I flung him quickly out the door, 'Good riddance!' was what I said.
    As he took a few steps from me –
        then once more my way did head!

FLIES

I bet no person living will disagree with me
When I declare the common fly is the worst pest there can be!
Flies love to play their games with us, they are skilled and so contrived,
    As they lie in wait for us to strike – then fly off before they've died!

Has anyone yet killed a fly as it sniggers on the sill?
Has anyone thought they would win when it sits so very still?
Do all of you react like me, 'Like a mad thing', some have said,
    As I reel about, that fly to clout, to strike him down quite dead!

It is rare to kill a fly – their name is very apt,
It's hard without a gadget to get them truly trapped.
Some years ago, perhaps today, flypapers graced most homes
    To catch flies on their sticky tongues, so they no longer roamed!

In olden days plants were the way to keep our fly at bay.
Basil and tansy, the whole mint family, did the trick old folk will say!
Elder festooned horse tack, nettles graced low ceilings,
    And camomile, and the oil of cloves were wiped upon the skin.

Modern ways will use fly sprays which knock them down en bloc!
A way so satisfying as they squirm there deep in shock!
But the only problem with this method are bodies a foot deep,
    Which require a brush and shovel to put them in a heap!

Another problem with the flies is their passion for new muck –
Which will create a nasty feeling as you watch them salve and suck!
The thought they might fly up and land upon your dinner plate
    Is a horrid, hateful, hideous thought, and not one to contemplate!

The breeds of flies are many - some Cluster, House and Horse.
Clusters are large, quite black and dense, they buzz a lot of course!
The House infests our food and drink, or anything left out,
    The Horse sucks every living thing - such as humans who will shout!

The Gnats flit in our faces in the warmness of the eve,
The Greenfly in the garden infest our veggie leaves.
The Crane can look quite menacing as he scoots around so blithe,
    And I would send each one of them to that fly morgue in the sky!

Unfortunately, I must admit to the intelligence of flies,
Not many things, not even cats, can claim such numerous lives!
Whoever else would have the nerve to go to all this caper
    For a possible fate of a huge headache from a swat with a newspaper!

Germs

The tiniest of our livestock is the unpretentious germ,
He is never seen by people, but into us his way he'll worm.
Because he is invisible, does not speak and is remote,
    Invariably humans use him as their own health scape-goat!
Think of your cold, now there's a germ, you caught him from somewhere.
If you've been sick, it's food poisoning, it's the gastro germ – beware!
Your leg has swollen from a cut, old germy's there inside,
    He's given you blood poisoning – do you know you could have died?

We're told to keep our worktops clean, 'Germs breed a lot you know!'
We're advised to bleach our dishcloths, 'There are germs on them which grow!'
Once underclothes were boiled each week, when intense heat would clear
    Those nasty, hateful, unseen things which to the skin adhere!
It is frightening where those germs will get, they manage it so well.
They immerse themselves in dirt and muck and then in us will dwell!
We know they visit smelly things, which to think of makes me heave
    And cause me to heed toilet signs to 'Wash your hands before you leave!'

The germ family is immensely vast, there must be relatives galore!
With family trees hundred miles long, and cousins by the score!
Perhaps each little sibling germ works for the family firm,
    From shopfloor to directorship, in departments all in turn!
The work which germ firms undertake must be highly organised,
Just imagine their commuting in this grand enterprise!
They must work on continuous shifts – germs do not stop at night,
    In fact their work is easiest then, 'cos sleeping people do not fight!

Brainy germs would take courses, a span of several years,
On the study of Germ Warfare, of which you will have heard!
The lesser germs will do piece-work on assembly lines and packing,
To supply germ packs to germ-free zones where germs are sorely lacking!
Germ export will be thriving, though not to countries which are cold,
Germs work much better in the heat, more so as they grow old!
I wonder where dead germs are laid, when they at last succumb
    To human medicines, which kill them by the ton!

I presume after a busy time germs need a holiday;
I have noticed that in summer time they seem to go away!
I wonder if they hibernate, go off to seek the sun,
Where in the heat, just for a treat, they inflict some gippy tum!
The thought of a germy future is hard to contemplate,
That germs infiltrate everything gets me in quite a state!
That they are with us, not seen, or felt, or even ever heard,
    Can make their existence dubious, and the whole germ thing
        absurd!

Nits

The day they found a nit at school on my daughter has remained
A time of shame and worry for a person unnit-trained!
    She was rushed home, then I rushed out to find treatment for a cure,
So that we who were nit-tainted would not infect those who were pure!

All those who've lived under nitty-shame know well the strong odour
Of the lotion which we're told to use when nits and such occur!
    It is so strong that its stench alone will adequately ensure
No nit will live upon our heads – 'cos the smell he won't endure!

The lotion wafts when we sit down, it tastes when we eat food,
It is not masked by onions, disinfectant or perfume!
    It remains with us in the atmosphere, it sleeps with us in bed,
But it's comforting at least to know, no nits will live upon our head!

Pure, nitless people will avoid those unclean with nits,
Ensure they become outcasts – and short-term nit-hermits!
    But a good side to this nitty tale which I confide to you
Is those who once avoided you – if with nits can be avoided too!

A Dog Tale

Our very small, smallholding, had a horse, a cow, some hens,
Some ducks and a few cockerels, who got fattened up in pens.
The cow she was a menace 'cos she chased all who came near,
    While a cockerel flew towards the throat should someone dare appear!
The ducks were very messy as they paddled in their mud,
The chickens very noisy as they clucked loud as they could,
The pigs would grunt and slosh a bit when their food arrived each day,
    But the horse who was the largest, could hardly raise a neigh!

Despite all this menagerie, it was a dog I really craved,
One who would sleep beside me when I was lonely and afraid.
But father thought all animals earned their living, stayed outside,
    So I gained a pair of rabbits, to whom I would confide!
Those rabbits were a menace, much more than any dog,
They hopped through any crevice - despite pailings made of log,
They gnawed lettuce, caused such chaos, so one was sent away,
    I didn't know where to at that time, and I still don't know today!

I've never had my little dog, I gained a husband, kids instead!
Yes! we had a pair of rabbits, which I mainly cleaned and fed.
A dog, we have not owned one - other things got in the way,
    But a hope remains that we might get that little dog one day.

THE EARTHWORM

I'd love to be a humble worm, and live deep underground,
    Within a hole so secret, I never could be found.
Within a world which is all mine, no-one could claim a bit,
    Where the light is not intrusive in passages unlit!

I'd live within the country – no town wormy I'd be.
    No concrete paths and stinking sewers, nor cars to bother me!
No busy parks, or clumsy feet to flatten my resolve,
    Or hardstandings where a lawn should be for burrows to evolve!

The country worm is better off, he can roam about at will,
    He can live within the fields and woods, or high upon the hill.
He can venture to the surface, penetrate the virgin land,
    And should he meet a woman worm – he can offer her his hand!

A lifestyle in the country does not mean the danger's less,
    When the risk from farm machinery is a constant source of stress!
The plough will delve relentlessly to destroy the family home,
    Does that farmer never think of orphaned worms left all alone?

Another cause for worry is the current garden craze,
    All that digging and that raking makes the mildest worm enraged!
Still worse is the lawn mower which cuts off heads and tails
    To leave the healthiest, fittest worm – a mass of worm entrails!

Also added to this peril are birds galore with beaks,
    Who when they spy a worm-like head, quick zoom down for a peek!
They seize and pull, and twist and heave, to get the body out –
    A worm victim has no chance against this feathered lout!

But left in peace the country worm has scruples not in town.
    The social gossip which he hears is not rocketed around!
Any scandal or adverse comment he keeps all to himself,
    Not networked on the underground as a source of social wealth!

A rural worm is not innocent, how ever can he be?
    When, through the heat of summer, to the country lovers flee!
They laugh and joke, and shift about - they never do stay still,
    Sometimes the earth is shook so much a wormy hole will fill!

One worm fed up with all this lark thought he would stop their game,
    So he headed to the surface in order to complain!
But when he spied what they were at, he withdrew in disbelief
    Worms you see are all the same - to him a great relief!

Yes! the lifestyle of an earthworm, can relate to human life,
    They might reside beneath the earth, but they share the same old strife!
They need some love, security, the chance to live in peace,
    And sadly it is us up here, who give them all their grief!

A Little Bird

If I were hatched a little bird I would be cheap to keep,
I would not need a hat or coat, or shoes upon my feet.
I'd not need gloves, warm socks, or coat, unless the sleeveless sort,
There'd be no risk of painful gout, so I could drink more port!

A skirt I might wear now and then, of course the feathered kind,
I would not need much make-up for my abundant quills to shine.
I might perhaps wear underwear – folk below might think that wise,
And perhaps a flying jacket, and some specs for beady eyes!

Nail varnish would not look amiss – I think it might enhance
The brightness of my shapely claws to give romance a chance!
A hairstyle would be not needed without a single strand,
And to brush and curl, blow-dry or swirl – would be hard without a hand!

Most happily I'd have no teeth, to ache, have filled, keep clean.
I'd gulp not chew, to get food through, so that should keep me lean.
I'd have no waist to keep all neat, no bust to lift or flout,
In flight it would be pleasant to let it all hang out!

Can wings get tennis elbow, or bird's legs housemaid's knee?
Can claws get corns or chilblains, or wings get blistery?
Can birds get colds without a nose, or little throats made sore,
No! chills would be improbable when a feathered coat is worn!

My cosy nest I'd intend to be environmentally sound,
In an affluent position, perched high above the ground.
In a sheltered, sunny aspect with a panoramic view
With insulation, solar heat, and wall-to-wall all through!

My grounds would stretch for acres and well-managed to produce
A host of various insects bred solely for my use!
I'd lease some land to other birds, small ones, those with respect,
Not ever stroppy, rude, blackbirds – their manners they neglect!

I'd call my home 'The Birds Eye View', not ever 'The Crows Nest'!
I'd employ someone to help me, to drive away the pests.
I'd holiday abroad each year, away from England's cold,
And I'd make a will should I be ill, but I intend to live 'til old!

Yes, a bird's life would just suit me, it seems to fit the bill,
Though I'd take a while to master the need to peck and kill.
I would of course cope with the change, up there in sky of blue,
Where I could judge all those below – from a bird's eye point of view!

THE RAT

We thought a mouse was in our shed, but in fact it was a rat!
It had taken all our dried broad beans from the tray wherein they sat.
Its home was in the trailer, among rubbish, twigs and gear -
    The thought of it just lurking there caused me to cringe with fear!

The first trap which we set that night was obviously too small.
He took the bait, escaped his fate, and poked fun at us all!
The larger trap gave him his end, but I did begin to think,
    'How sad if he was a mummy rat, with ratlets bare and pink!'

I remember quite a long time back when a rat was in our home,
It was a rocking, rolling rat, with a beat which made us groan!
Each night as we lay still in bed, it thumped and bumped around
    As we shouted out from down below to quieten Ratty down!

We duly called in Rat Man, 'Come quickly, please', we said,
'Some vermin are within this house, we can hear them when in bed!'
He came quite soon, a happy soul, to fathom paths and trails,
    Then he left some bait, which rave-rat ate, and peaceful nights prevailed!

After a while a nasty smell pervaded through the house,
We wondered what it might be – was it, this time, a mouse?
But, 'No', rat expert told us, 'that smell is a dead rat'!
    The pong would go, although quite slow, so we resigned ourselves to that!

A year or so, just after some more piping we installed
Within the marital bedroom, underneath the flooring boards,
Well, I expect you've guessed it – we found our Ratty's hide
    Beneath those varnished bedroom boards. And yes! it was my side!

Ratty was shrunk and shrivelled up beside those nice warm pipes.
He must have been intelligent, for he knew just what he liked!
Surrounding him possessions gleaned while still alive on earth,
    Some paper, a small piece of rag, some old beads of no worth!

To think that we and Ratty slept so close for that time,
That we all breathed the same old air in our ignorance sublime!
As we snuggled up in bed above, you curled your tail in yours,
    Oh! I never would have slept a wink, had I known all this before!

No, I never will get over it – the thought of Ratty there!
He must have heard our every word, and knew that I was scared.
I bet he made that awful noise just simply out of spite,
    Thinking, 'If they complain again – then they shall stay awake all night!'

Fish

I'd hate to be a poor old fish who lives in water deep,
Who has no arms, no hands or legs, and certainly no feet.
Who has no hair, or ears like us, nor has he got a nose,
Whose body is quite boring when he cannot wear bright clothes.

    All day our fish just gulps and stares – what is there else to do?
    All day he lies immersed in wet – now is that good for you?
    He does not talk or make a sound – just blows bubbles here and there,
    He really is a sad old thing – life for him is far from fair!

Devoid of limbs, activities are reduced beyond belief,
He cannot cook, or chew like us, though fish do have some teeth.
The only time he'll see a plate is when he's lying there,
Smothered in sauce, parsley of course, served up to us with flair!

The saddest thing about no limbs is that a fish can't nurse her young
Not in her arms like human babes as we up here have done!
No pushchair to be wheeled around – that would float up to the top,
Or even potty train babe fish – I suppose theirs sinks and rots!

    Many fish are white, or pale at least, because a fish can take no sun.
    Some might be pink, though salmon's red, which is a bit more fun!
    When fish are caught, gutted, and cooked, most seem a shade of grey,
    On sale at the fishmongers – they're off-colour in a tray.

Fish lie in dread of being caught by net or horrid hook,
So perhaps it's well, tales they can't tell and write them in a book.
Just imagine that sharp cruel hook hitched in your mouth like that,
Or even worse, their feline foe – our friendly tabby cat!

They'd be better with defences, like knuckles, feet and nails,
To protect them if in danger, when swimming fast has failed.
Their lives would be much safer could they punch, and kick and scratch,
And also a much fairer and more equal match!

   Yes, fish have got a raw deal – they're better off when cooked!
   When hot with lemon slices they are not overlooked!
   Down in the murk, without much work, they stand no chance of fame,
   But up on earth we love them – fried, battered, poached or plain!

Fox and Hounds, or the Superiority of Nature Against the Fallibility of Humanity

The myth about fox hunting should come out to be aired.
That the fox and hound are really friends should be finally declared!
    That these two are the closest pals who despise the likes of you
Is well known in their circles, so humans should know it too!

As humans we all like to think it's hounds against the foe,
We ride along and sabotage, fired with this tale of woe!
    But in reality the fox and pack mock us behind our backs
And arrange some devious little games designed to make us crack!

Both parties feel that this hunting lark has got well out of hand,
A day for them so pleasant before the coming of 'the band'.
    Now that the 'rights' and huntspeople are playing their own game
The fox and hounds twice-weekly bet has slid right down the drain!

It is at least twelve years or more since they decided on their scheme,
Where they bet on the number of huntsmen they could persuade into the stream,
    Where the winning treat for the hound pack was a party shared by all –
And the cash gained for the foxes went towards their Christmas Ball!

The recent week of cold and wet allowed their game a break
Which caused them to anticipate a hefty betting stake!
    So a preformed plan caused them combined to widen out the stream,
Which was camouflaged most carefully in various shades of green!

Young foxy says he'll run across the field just over there!
The hounds say they will head him off so he must be prepared!
    The Elder fox says Grandad will confuse the huntsmen's trail
And tempt those 'rights' folk another way if Head hound will help him there!

The day was most successful when twelve slipped in murky wet,
A good day out for both fox and hound and a source of merriment!
    The winning decision was hard to make but in the end it was a draw
As they agreed between them that they had enjoyed it all!

It was decided that a combined meal would complete their happy time.
Perhaps some fowl, nothing which growled – farm hens would just be fine!
    They drank some milk, and sucked some eggs, toasted what they'd achieved,
And laughed at all those silly folk, whom they had just deceived!

(This is simply an observation. It is not intended as a comment either way on the issue of hunting.)

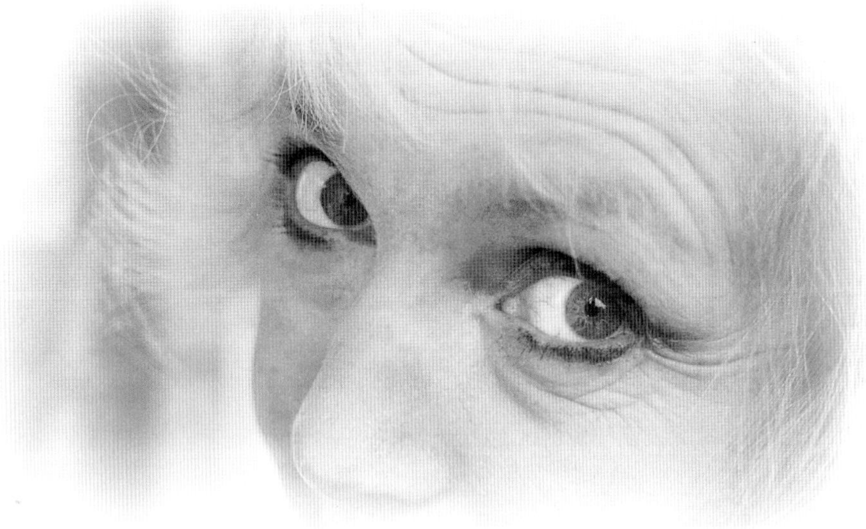

Miscellaneous

The following is a hotch-potch, those things of this and that.
They are a verbal mish-mash all jumbled in a hat.
They are bits and bobs, a wish-wash, of knick-knacks – which don't compare,
A bodged-up mess, of odds and sods which are neither here nor there.

Inspiration for this jumbled pile came from experience,
The one I wrote on hoses – the result of being drenched!
The one concerning Toilet Rolls because I thought it mean
Not to praise something used by all, which we constantly demean!

The one about the lavatory will touch the heart of those
Who cannot embark upon a trip without the urge to go!
The feel the need immediately they emerge from their front door,
So back they go another time – then en route they'll look for more!

The rhyme on Mr Dustbin is a tribute to a chap
Who has always been there for us to fill with this and that!
He stands outside in rain and snow, to await our every whim,
But we just take him for granted, as we stuff him to the brim!

The rhyme on Light, because there is too much, and the dark is very good
For dreaming dreams, and thinking, to immerse within a mood.
For hiding, and observing things not obvious in the light,
Which become as clear as crystal in the velvet of the night.

I thank you all for reading this, you really have been good!
I've enjoyed myself just doing it, but I thought maybe I would!
My little break is over now – back to real life and hard graft,
And to some semblance of sanity – which I must resume at last!

The Lavatory

As long as I remember, I've loved the lavatory.
  I like to know there is one, and where it is to be.
If in a room with others, or in a small room on its own,
  If near and if convenient, so I won't need to roam!

When we go out, I worry until I've spotted one in town,
  I scan the signs for 'Toilet' before I settle down!
When I know that there is one the urge then goes away,
  If I have not sought one out - then I want to go all day!

I think a lavatory's special because we lacked one for so long.
  Our home had just an Elsan which emitted a strong pong!
It needed frequent emptying, which was a tiresome chore
  Of a lengthy carry down the path - not a quick fling out the door!

Our cheap blue plastic bucket was much cleaner but a curse,
  It was difficult to sit on - left a ring which made it worse!
We bore it over two whole years while we made a sceptic tank,
  Then we put it in the garage, where it mouldered, stayed, and stank!

Our brand new pampas toilet was christened with acclaim,
  I was the first to use it, so I gave to it my name!
It was to us so much a joy, no-one will ever know,
  A comfy seat, a proper flush - a pleasure just to go!

The addition of an upstairs caused us to think again.
  In the deep, dark night do we venture down, or struggle to refrain?
With visions of old stiffened limbs we installed one within reach,
  So at last, and for the first time, we have a whole loo each!

The Toilet Roll

A rhyme about a toilet roll is not the lowest of the low,
We won't investigate its habits, where it's been – where it can go!
Instead we see its cultural side, its emotions deep inside,
Away from its main function,
          for which we creep away and hide!

The toilet roll is a soft old thing, well at least it is today!
Its forefather was the newspaper – harder, strung up some way!
Then came along the Izal – slick, smooth and very small,
The modern one we have today,
          I feel is the nicest of them all!

Toilet rolls are sociable, they like to roam in gangs,
To travel widely in large packs like close-knit family clans!
To display themselves in carriers, upon which we all will see
Their name proudly emblazoned,
          Tissue – Soft and Luxury!

Rolls proudly boast their thickness, their size, and even length!
Ours here is only two-ply, though forty metres in extent!
But it still brags three hundred sheets, we have some usage there
When we can visit many times –
          without the need to share!

Most toilet rolls are subtly tinged to match a house décor,
It makes them quickly feel at home in the room they're destined for!
Some purchasers will thoughtlessly place orange rolls in loos of pink.
These should be left without a roll –
          that would make them sit and think!

The difference with our tissues is they do a whole lot more
Than the function already mentioned, which we design them for!
Mine wipe my nose, my eyes, my mouth, they tackle things at home,
In fact I feel quite ill at ease
        without mine when I roam!

The roll's vast versatility is reflected in my bag.
I have one in there tucked away – it's well travelled and jet lagged!
But while mine is pink, they could be white, blue, mauve, or green,
Their extensive range of colours
        will match with any theme!

A sadness I find quite hard to take is a tissue's final end,
When after all their vital work they are not treated as a friend!
Had someone else done the same for you – and done the things they do,
Would you as a decent kindly chap,
        just flush them down the loo?

I feel a tribute to our roll would be, The Order of the Rear!
So at last to recognise their worth, and their importance made quite clear!
After all when things are getting scarce what is it that we all do?
We rush around to stock well up
        with rolls to see us through!

HOSES AND PIPES

The hose it is so wayward, it goes it's own sweet way,
When sometimes straight, obedient, or bent in disarray.

When it snakes and twists, or kinks and bends, to halt what is within,
Or spurts a leak – just for a treat – to drench us to the skin!

Hoses are long, they can be short, but their temperament is renowned
For their pleasure when they trip us up, or their skill when wrestling down!

To raise tempers and blood pressures is their target of the day,
To cause a general chaos – and often great dismay!

So different is the stalwart pipe – so solid and contained.
He's strong and straight like a Roman road, with a thoughtful logical brain.

He stays where he is hauled and set – to move he never would,
In fact if he attempted, it is doubtful if he could!

Pipes mostly are great loners - they do not gad about!
They're not keen on hose frivolity, drinking or going out!

They are refined, smooth dressers, good mannered, with good taste,
Pillars of society and the backbone of our waste!

Those hoses which are above the earth claim much the healthier share
As they convey air, liquid dust, within domestic care!

They accommodate our washers, our vacuums and our showers,
In fact when they choose to behave, they can save us many hours!

Up here on top their lighter work will give a good lifestyle,
Unlike the poor old pipe below in the dark for mile on mile!

Even when old and cracked a bit, a hose will still perform –
When a simple amputation means he's shorter, but reborn!

The honest pipe is lonely in his home deep underground.
He cannot see the world outside – he just hears some muffled sound!

Sadly even when here on top he is rarely ever free
From employment used in effluence – connected to a lavatory!

Mr Dustbin

The role of Mr Dustbin is to accept discarded things,
Not precious goods like heirlooms, money, or diamond rings!
    For him it is sad items who in the depths of deep despair
Know that when finally their end appears – a Mr Dustbin will be there!

Visitors are all made welcome, no-one is turned away,
Some reside for a few hours, some will lodge for several days!
    They all await a Council cart, which will transport them to
Some large tip in the countryside to be covered from our view!

Crammed under Mr Dustbin's lid, refuse is sad indeed,
They know at last their time has come, so no use to cry and plead!
    Wrappings assume a screwed-up state, an old shoe down at heel,
Old letters which are written off, and orange peel will not appeal!

Once refuse was a varied bunch, a mixture of all breeds,
Although should they not hit it off, this to arguments might lead!
    Like a tissue used on an affluent nose who'd recoil from bags from
        fish!
Or a Royal Doulton broken plate who'd avoid some cracked old dish!

Mr Dustbin's role in recent times has undergone an innate change,
When environmental issues have caused a segregation in his range!
    Some items, which were hastily thrust into his loving care,
Are now kept back from others, to be carted off elsewhere!

These cast-off, élite, recycling bits are slightly better fixed,
When despite bashing and scalping they have at least been picked!
    They too are washed so to be sweet for their journey to the Plant,
Where with luck and searching they might find friends, sisters, brothers,
        aunts!

Some might discover long-lost friends, jars might with lids unite!
Bags, cartons, and take-aways complain about their plight!
    Nice things like used-up talcum tins aid to enhance the air,
But in the end they're all down-and-outs with a future they must share!

Even genial Mr Dustbin is resigned to a big change,
To a possible redundancy through the encroaching Wheelie range!
    Refuse company directors think mobile and big is best,
So they've consigned their smaller dustbins to a long unwelcome rest!

The upstart, upfront Wheelie Bin has claimed the people's doors,
So sad for Mr Dustbin to see him pop up more and more!
    A Dustbin retired is a sorry sight when he's packed with this and that,
And devoid of regular visits – except by next door's cat!

His lonely life could last for years because he is so good
At providing a container which is mouse-proof for pet food!
    But until his time to go arrives, I bet you'll wait a bit
Before you'll see a Mr Dustbin being carted to the tip!

LIGHT

Remember when our roads were dark and we groped within the gloom,
When people did not use house lights in each and every room?
When in the dark the stars above were magical and bright?
Then for me it was a pleasure to go out into the night!
Today it seems that everyone wants lights just everywhere,
Their eyes cannot see anything because of all the glare.
A while ago a simple torch led us whence we would wend,
Or we went out without a light, because darkness was our friend.
If you can find some happy spot where light does not intrude,
Notice your calm and wonder, and the difference in your mood.
Look to the trees, the sky, the shapes, their colours and the sights,
And you might just return back home – to switch off all those lights!

Time

Where do all our hours go when we put clocks back each year?
Do they return to the same old place to families held dear?
Do they come back again in Spring to be sent forward as before?
Or do we have a younger bunch to last us 'til the fall?

When time flies whence does it fly - is it somewhere far away?
When it stands still, is it static - when it goes where does it stay?
When happy does it dance and sing - when, bad break rules and law?
If we take time, to take time out, will a good time be had by all?

Once upon a time I had more time, it was mine to have and use.
As I grew, my time grew short, it was lessened like a fuse!
In time to come, my time will come, I will have had my time,
Until that time, I'll make some time, to ensure a real good time!

Dreams

The book in front of me today is all about our dreams,
It reveals their hidden secrets, their meanings and such things.
   It indicates our inner thoughts to reveal the way we are,
That certain dreams mean this or that, what we think, and what we are!
I wake up now to think my dreams while they appear quite clear,
Which means I suffer loss of sleep when those dreams do interfere.
   But should I sleep, then I'll miss out on what might help when I'm awake,
So daily I am all worn out, so advice on dreams I won't forsake!

'Abandonment' seen within a dream can mean quite different things.
It means I either gain a lot, or I lose most everything!
   'Abundance' means I build a stock for leaner times in store,
'Acceptance' is a love success – or a wide financial door!
'Chastisement' means finances will take an upward surge,
'Humility' is a warning from overconfidence and verve!
   'Hysterics' will, without care, mean substantial business loss,
Which will create 'Annoyance', and 'Hurdles', which I must cross!

A man who dreams he's 'Hen-pecked', should hold his temper tight!
A woman who is 'Proposed to' will find her 'Mr Right'!
   A 'Valentine' with lace, perfume, will claim for me a kiss,
A 'Wedding' is the forerunner of happiness not to miss!
The dreams of 'Little Children' means a family of some stance,
A 'Boy' is a good omen to indicate advance!
   A 'Girl' means love, when to me she sets a standard of my taste
Of the 'Happiness' which I must use and never put to waste!

So there you have a sample of what you'll find inside,
A muddle of those daily thoughts which creep away to hide.
   Which in the night burst out to form a picture in the mind,
Which may be bright and vibrant, but are not always kind!
I shall not tonight remain awake to think this muddle through –
I feel dreams are a waste of time since my confidence to you!
   Instead I'll take my dreams forthwith in the spirit they are meant –
As a nightly entertainment when relaxed, in bed, content!

GRASS

If nature had a medal for perseverance and for pluck,
    The humble grass should get it as its only piece of luck!
No other plant is treated in such diverse and cruel ways,
    When it's trod on, pulled up, cut off, and given up to graze!

A grass knows there is not much hope, as he peeps above the ground,
    Quite pensive and so fearful - shoots alert for any sound.
When heavy feet and blunted blades crush down and shoots do hack,
    And other nasty, stinky things slosh down to give him loads of flack!

The élitist grass class system will combine to cause grass rifts
    Between finer genteel grasses, and those hard, wild unclipped!
The finer grasses so dislike the wider coarser breeds,
    That they make sure they are rooted out, treated just like weeds!

Should I be found to be a grass, I'd choose a nibble not a scalp!
    A game maybe of football, though goal grass might make me yelp!
I would not mind the honour of the Wembley hallowed ground,
    Or a racecourse as 'good going', on which winning hooves could pound!

A further grassy element is racism, which is bad
    When a grass is banned from borders, unless some special lad!
When labelled 'couch', he's tortured and burned, which this very day
    Should be reported immediately - to the grass RSPCA!

Equality for any grass is when the silent snow arrives
    To cover all, of whatever class, in white, just as a bride.
Then fine or broad, or long or short, all grasses hide in peace,
    As every grass activity is forced temporarily to cease!

The Force of Gravity

If I was born Creator, I'd have left out gravity,
   It is the greatest menace for folks like you and me!
      It is dangerous and restrictive, when we are all pulled down –
         From the moment we arrive on earth
            we head straight for the ground!

Gravity makes wobbly toddlers and babies slip and fall,
   Tiddly teenagers topple, sportsmen miss their ball!
      Racehorses knock down fences – the desire to mountaineer,
         And we all know when we're getting old,
            because drooping does appear!

Gravity makes ageing worse when it encourages things to drop!
   To give more chins, and bags on eyes, and busts which need a prop!
      It makes waists slump, stomachs drop down, all weight goes to the knee,
         And some bits viewed once easily –
            become impossible to see!

No gravity would send tears up, make-up would cease to streak.
   Eyelids would never ever droop, and chins drop towards feet!
      Our mouths would always be turned up, we never would look sad,
         Our hair might tend to stand on end –
            but then some hairstyles always have!

Gravity is so unhealthy – just survey the common cold,
   Your nose it runs, so you blow and wipe to try to stem the flow!
      Your sneeze goes up, then falls again to spray all those in sight,
         Did you realise that this gravity
            will cause snuffling tonight?

If things went up, we'd have a chance to dodge safe underneath.
  We would not need to weigh ourselves, or walk upon our feet!
    We'd save on shoes, socks, trousers, when as free and light as air
      We could rise over all those disliked -
        if we weighted them somewhere!

No gravity could cause problems - skirts might not be advised!
  All underclothes would be a must to shield from prying eyes!
    We'd no doubt lose belongings, they'd fly, get muddled up,
      And a drink of tea or coffee
        not stay down in the cup!

Sports people, like high jumpers, would not be seen again
  Aeroplanes not need their runways, nor umbrellas screen from rain!
    Our homes might not be best with bricks, they'd fly up in the air,
      And lids would go on everything
        to keep contents in there!

I think we'll stick with gravity, the risk appears too great,
  We'll make it from this moment before it is too late!
    To imagine this around the world, and the chaos it would bring
      Makes gravity the better bet -
        since we're used to the whole thing!

Not The Bitter End

Why must the end be bitter, I wish this to be sweet,
   To be a special goodbye to be savoured as a treat.
As a conclusion to a memorable meal, a pleasure on the tongue,
   As an indulgence and an apt reward now all the work is done.
This end shall be as treacle, not as lemon or tart lime,
   As jam sauce over creamy rice, which to diets is a crime,
As several squares of chocolate, not grapefruit or rhubarb,
   As toffee sticky on the teeth, not cider apples hard.
As honey eaten from the comb, a glass of sweet, white wine,
   To complement the completion of my thoughts put into rhyme.

THE LAST

At Last!